TEACHER
Bible Readers Series

A Study of Romans

GOOD NEWS
FOR
GOD'S PEOPLE

Douglas E. Wingeier

Abingdon Press / Nashville

Hope for the Future
A Study of Romans

Copyright © 1993 by Cokesbury.

Revised Edition Copyright © 2000 by Abingdon Press.

Lessons are based on the International Sunday School Lessons for Christian Teaching, copyright © 1990 by the Committee on the Uniform Series.

ISBN 0-687-08219-6

00 01 02 03 04 05 06 07 08 09—10 9 8 7 6 5 4 3 2 1
Manufactured in the United States of America.

CONTENTS

PETER, PAUL, AND THE CHURCH AT ROME

By Harold C. Perdue

"To all God's beloved in Rome, who are called to be saints" (Romans 1:7): So Paul addressed his letter to the Christians in Rome. What do we know about this group of believers in the capital of the Empire? How did their fellowship begin? What was Peter's relationship with them? What was Paul's? What was the role of the church in Rome in later years?

Our knowledge of the early years of Christianity in Rome is limited. We learn a little from the Book of Acts and from the Letter to the Romans. Some secular writings preserve indirect references. Ancient traditions about Peter, Paul, and the Roman church were remembered and written down by later Christian scholars. That is, writings of Christian leaders more than 150 years after the time of the New Testament provide us with anecdotes and legends concerning the role of the two apostles in the capital city. These ancient traditions are not verifiable history, however.

In sum, much of our "knowledge" of the early Roman church is constructed from surmise, calculations, theories, and educated guess work. A picture of the Roman church emerges, but it is an obscure one.

HOW DID THE CHURCH IN ROME BEGIN?

During the century before Jesus, Jews scattered to various parts of the world. Many went to Rome. One estimate is that more than twenty thousand Jews lived in the capital city during the first century. Eventually, there were thirteen synagogues in Rome, although it is not clear that all thirteen existed during the time of Peter and Paul.

Early Christianity was nurtured by the synagogue. According to the Book of Acts, when Paul came to a town, he spoke in the synagogue first. Thus many of the first groups of Christians participated in the synagogues. It is reasonable to assume that this was also the case in Rome, that is, that the Christian church began as a movement within the synagogues of the city.

We have no evidence about the actual beginning of the church in Rome. Some have taken Acts 2:10 as a clue. When the disciples were filled with the Holy Spirit on Pentecost, among the crowd that gathered were visitors to Jerusalem from Rome. They are identified as "both Jews and proselytes." The Acts account does not state that these people carried the new faith back to Rome, however.

One church tradition proposes that Barnabas founded the church in Rome. Barnabas had been a companion of Paul. He plays a vital role in the account of Paul's mission in Chapters 13, 14, and 15 of Acts. The two went their separate ways after a dispute over John Mark (Acts 15:39). Paul was opposed to Mark's return after Mark had deserted the two missionaries. Paul and Barnabas separated, and Barnabas took Mark with him. The Book of Acts does not refer to either John Mark or Barnabas by name after the fifteenth chapter. However, some have conjectured that Barnabas and John Mark made their way to Rome.

John Mark is thought to be the writer of the Gospel of Mark. One Christian tradition places Mark in Rome when he wrote his Gospel. This tradition also holds that Mark built his narrative on the recollections of Peter. Placing Mark in Rome with Barnabas and Peter (1 Peter 5:13) supports the thought that Barnabas was the founder of the church there.

If we assume that Barnabas and Mark did journey to Rome, then we may also assume that in the Roman synagogues they would have found people who had received reports of Peter's Pentecost sermon in

Jerusalem. The number of believers may have grown until Christians were an identifiable community, as when Paul writes to them. On this understanding, Peter and Paul would arrive later and church growth would continue under their leadership.

WHAT WAS PETER'S ROLE IN THE CHURCH IN ROME?

Peter's relation to the church in Rome is difficult to ascertain. There is no report in the New Testament pertaining to a visit by Peter to Rome, no hint that Peter was there at any time during the two years Paul was under house arrest. Moreover, Paul's letter to the Romans has no reference to Peter. Yet according to Christian traditions, Peter played a crucial role in the church in Rome.

One tradition states that Peter arrived in Rome as early as A.D. 45 and completed his ministry there. First Peter 5:13 sends greetings from "Babylon." In the cryptic language of the New Testament, "Babylon" is thought to refer to Rome itself.

Clement of Rome, writing at the end of the first century concerning Paul's martyrdom, also commented on Peter. Clement wrote, "He [Peter] suffered not one or two but many trials, and having thus given his testimony went to the glorious place that was his due." Ignatius [ig-NAY-shus] of Antioch, at the beginning of the second century, wrote a letter to the Roman Christians. He referred to Paul and Peter directing the church in Rome. Thus, within fifty years of the deaths of Peter and Paul, both men were associated with the Roman church.

We discover more definite references to Peter and Paul in Christian literature from later in the second century. Dionysius [digh-uh-NISH-ee-uhs], a bishop of Corinth, writing about A.D. 175, notes that Peter and Paul founded both the Corinthian and the Roman churches. Irenaeus [EYE-ruh-nee-uhs] writes about the same time of Peter and Paul both preaching at Rome and laying the foundation of the church there. Tertullian [tuhr-TUL-yen], near the beginning of the third century, refers to three martyrs in Rome, including Peter and Paul. Clement of Alexandria, a contemporary of Tertullian, places the writing of First Peter at Rome. Origen, living in Asia Minor during the first half of the third century, wrote that Peter was crucified head down at Rome. And Gaius of Rome wrote that one could see the monuments to Peter and Paul on Vatican Hill and the Ostian Way in Rome. Gaius referred to the two apostles as "those who founded this church."

Most of these references are reported in a history of the church by Eusebius [you-SEE-bee-uhs] of Caesarea. This church historian lived between A.D. 260 and A.D. 340. While each of these recollections probably contains some legendary elements, they may be founded on factual events. However, even though Peter's influence on the church in Rome is evident in much early church history, we cannot determine with certainty the extent or the length of his association with the church.

WHAT WAS PAUL'S RELATION TO THE CHURCH IN ROME?

Paul's relationship with the church in Rome is more widely attested. The Book of Acts and the Letter to the Romans provide direct evidence of his presence and ministry in Rome.

The word *Rome* occurs nine times in the New Testament: six times in the Book of Acts, two times in Paul's letter to the Romans, and one time in Second Timothy. One of the occurrences in Acts refers to the expulsion of Aquila [AK-wi-luh] and Prisca, along with other Jews, from the city by the Emperor Claudius (probably around A.D. 49). This expulsion may have been because of controversy in the synagogues surrounding the claim that Jesus was the Messiah. Two of the occurrences of the word *Rome* are from comments by Paul about plans to visit the city on his way to the West. And two more are in the narrative about Paul's arrival in Rome, found in Acts 28.

Precise dates for Paul's letter to Rome and for his visit are difficult to determine. Paul's death probably occurred between A.D. 60 and A.D. 65. If Romans was written in 56–57, Paul probably arrived in Rome two to four years later. Considering his two years of house arrest, his martyrdom would have taken place about 62 or 63.

Another tradition holds that Paul was released and traveled to Spain. In this account, he was later arrested again, charged, and returned to Rome. He then died in the persecution of A.D. 64–65 along with Peter. This second theory depends strongly on a statement in 2 Timothy 4. There Paul refers to how everyone deserted him during his first defense, but God was with him. "So I was rescued from the lion's mouth" (2 Timothy 4:17).

There is no definitive answer to the question of the date and circumstances of Paul's martyrdom. We have sufficient evidence to believe that Paul was actively involved with the Christians in Rome, and we can believe that his outstanding preaching attracted many converts there. His influence on Rome was as extensive as it was on other cities.

One tradition maintains that Paul wrote letters to the Philippians, to the Colossians, to Philemon, and to the Ephesians from Rome. However, there is considerable disagreement about the place from which Paul wrote these letters. Nonetheless, in Colossians 4:11, Paul refers to three fellow workers, including Mark, the cousin of Barnabas; and Mark's association with the church in Rome has been reinforced by this reference.

Philippians may also have been written from Rome. Philippians 1:15-18b refers to some who preach Christ to support Paul, while others preach Christ to afflict Paul in his imprisonment. The reference in 2 Timothy 4:17 indicates that Paul was not supported by many Christians during his stay in Rome. This could refer to that same rivalry. In Philippians 4:18, Paul thanks the Philippians for the gifts that sustain him. It has been surmised that the Philippians sent support through one Epaphroditus [i-paf-ruh-DIGH-tuhs]. The implication is that the local support was so limited that Paul needed the assistance of his friends in other places. Philippians 4:22 gives greetings from Caesar's household. This verse can be interpreted to refer to any officials of the Empire anywhere. However, it may refer to those in the government in Rome itself.

Paul's association with Rome is further attested by the lengthy list of persons in Romans 16. Paul names twenty-seven different people. Some Bible scholars suggest that Paul would not know that many people in a church he had never visited. These scholars speculate that this chapter is part of another letter, somehow misplaced within the Letter to the Romans. However, it is not unreasonable to accept these greetings as genuine.

Prisca and Aquila are mentioned in Romans 16:3. We learn from Acts 18 that Prisca and Aquila lived in Corinth after leaving Rome. They are also greeted in 2 Timothy 4:19, while they send greetings in 1 Corinthians 1:19. Prisca and Aquila obviously lived in several places. As Claudius was dead by the time of the letter to Rome, the couple may have returned to Rome to reconstruct their lives there. Association with one church does not exclude persons from association with another church, even one in a distant city.

The Letter to the Romans includes greetings from eight persons accompanying Paul. These eight might have told Paul about people he should greet in Rome even if he did not know them personally. It is reasonable to assume some of the eight were from Rome themselves.

There may have been more than one gathering of Christians in Rome. In the list of twenty-seven persons, three couples are named. Church groups may have met in their homes. Paul names one person and that person's mother; he names a man and his sister; he names two different households. Paul also greets five individuals grouped together and the saints "with them." He wanted to establish his friendship with and interest in the Christians of Rome, for he wanted them to be ready to receive him when he arrived.

It is clear that Paul did travel to Rome. While there (for at least two years), he preached to as many people as he could. No matter how many persons Paul knew in Rome, no matter if he was released and then returned or was imprisoned until his death, Paul's influence on the Roman church was profound and enduring.

WHAT HAPPENED TO THE CHURCH IN ROME AFTER THE DEATHS OF PETER AND PAUL?

As noted above, our knowledge of the early church in Rome is limited. It is as difficult to piece together a clear picture of the story of the church as it is to discover the details of Peter and/or Paul's interaction with it. We do know that the Roman church continued to grow. Living at the center of the Empire, the Christians in Rome assumed a role of leadership. Although Christianity flourished in many major cities throughout the Empire, Rome ascended to a role of prominence. The power of the church in Rome grew slowly over the first few centuries. However, by the fourth century, when the Emperor Constantine granted full benevolence to Christians, the prestige of the Roman church was clear.

The church of Rome did not develop a distinctive theological perspective before Constantine. The popular emphasis was on the choice between the way of righteousness and the way of evil. The intellectual interests of the church revolved more around issues of ecclesiastical order, examining questions of rigidity and flexibility. Facing repeated instances of persecution from emperors opposed to the claims of the faith, the Christians in Rome drew courage from those they understood to be martyrs for the cause of Christ, including Peter and Paul.

Chapter One

SAVED BY FAITH

PURPOSE

To affirm that through faith we participate in God's salvation

BIBLE PASSAGE

Romans 1:1, 3-17
Background: Romans 1:1-17

> ### CORE VERSE
> I am not ashamed of the gospel; it is the power of God for salvation to everyone who has faith.
> (Romans 1:16)

GET READY

■ The theme of the study on Romans we are beginning is "Good News for God's People." As you begin preparation, pause to think about the segment of God's people that makes up your group. Hold these persons up in prayer, one by one, remembering the good news that each needs to hear as these lessons unfold.

If you have time, read or skim through all eight lessons to get a sense of the progression of ideas. Reflect on the themes—salvation by faith, God's gift of a Son, reconciliation with God, deliverance from sin and death, Christ's resurrected glory, and new life in Christ expressed in service.

Read the Scripture passage for this lesson; then think through and write down your own answers to the questions posed in the lesson in the student book.

BIBLE BACKGROUND

■ Before beginning this study, read the entire Book of Romans. Doing so will help you understand how the themes raised in this lesson and in subsequent lessons relate to the primary issues and ideas presented in the letter as a whole.

Paul probably wrote this letter to the churches at Rome during the three months he spent in Corinth (Acts 20:1-3) in the winter of A.D. 56–57, just before he left on his journey to Jerusalem to deliver the offering that had been collected for Christians there (Romans 15:28). In the last chapter he commends Phoebe (Romans 16:1), who was from the town of Cenchreae [SEN-kruh-ee] near Corinth, to the Romans' hospitality when she arrives in their city. He also sends greetings from his host, Gaius of Corinth (Romans 16:23).

The immediate reason for the letter is to ask the Roman house churches to aid Paul's mission to Spain (Romans 15:24, 28). Because believers in all places are one in salvation through Christ, Paul urges them to unite in supporting the proclamation of the good news, which is "the power of God for salvation to everyone" (Romans 1:16). Paul's exposition of the theme of justification by faith is the theological foundation for this evangelistic mission. Thus he wants the Romans to understand and to support his position.

Unlike Paul's other letters, Romans is sent to a church he did not found. Therefore he devotes verses 1-15 of Chapter 1 to introducing himself and to presenting his credentials. Then Paul uses verses 16-17 to summarize the gospel he is called to preach, which he expounds in the rest of the letter.

Romans 1:1-2. Paul begins his self-introduction by saying he is called to be a servant, an apostle, and one set apart. His calling came directly from Christ at the time of his conversion (Acts 22:1-16; 26:12-18). The word translated *servant* literally means *slave*. In imperial Rome a slave was not necessarily in a "servile" position; one could be a slave in the sense of being a representative, as in being a slave or representative of Caesar. Thus Paul represents Christ as an *apostle*, that is, as "one sent with a message on a mission." Paul's mission is to proclaim the gospel, the good news of God, the focus of the epistle. The word *God* appears over 150 times in Romans, that is, about once every 46 words. Romans is basically a book about God.

Verses 3-4. After the word *Son*, these verses are taken from an early Christian creed. We can infer from the mention of David that this creed was developed by Jewish Christians, although the references to "the spirit of holiness" and "resurrection from the dead" would appeal to Gentiles. Paul's point: Jesus the Messiah has both the historical and the spiritual qualities to be the universal Savior.

Verses 5-6. Paul stresses "our" (verse 4) and "we" (verse 5), suggesting that the authority from Christ to proclaim the good news to the Gentiles is shared with all who accept his call "to belong to Jesus Christ." All Christians are missionaries and/or evangelists.

Verse 7. The letter is addressed to "all God's beloved in Rome." Roman Christians were probably dispersed over several house churches. Paul tells these believers that God cares for them all and wants them to love one another and to live faithful, dedicated lives. He offers his standard greeting, stressing the grace and peace of the priestly blessing in Numbers 6:25-26. Both benedictions have been widely used throughout church history.

Verses 8-10. Having established his apostolic credentials and given his greeting, Paul now praises the Roman Christians for their faith, assures them of his prayerful concern, and states his intention to pay them a visit. The "all of you" in verse 8 may be intended to include both those still committed to observance of traditional Jewish patterns of worship and conduct and those who felt no obligation to conform to Jewish calendar and law. In Chapters 14 and 15, these persons are referred to as the "weak" and the "strong," respectively.

Serving God "with my spirit" (verse 9) is another way of saying "with all my heart or might." Paul held nothing back in his devotion to his Lord. As the Romans cannot actually see him, Paul calls God as his witness that he continually prays for their well-being. His missionary plan includes a visit to Rome and then to Spain (Romans 15:23-24); but he is waiting for God to open the way, and other priorities keep interfering (verse 13).

Verses 11-13. The purpose of Paul's proposed visit is both to help strengthen the Roman Christians in the faith and to be encouraged himself as well. He recognizes that both he and they have need of spiritual power and stimulation from the outside and that the Christians in Rome can teach him as well as learn from him. Moreover, as Paul hopes eventually to go beyond Rome to Spain, he probably plans to use Rome as a base from which he can draw spiritual support. Since Paul is writing from Corinth, the "spiritual gift" (verse 11) could well refer to the discussion of spiritual gifts in 1 Corinthians 12 and 13, with emphasis on the primacy of love. There may be some hard feelings among the Roman Christians, now embroiled in controversy over observance of the law. The obstacles to Paul's earlier arrival are not mentioned here but can be seen in 2 Corinthians 11:24-28. He has won Gentile converts in other places and longs to reap a similar harvest in Rome, a Gentile city and the capital of the Mediterranean world. Paul's reference to "brothers and sisters" recalls Jesus words: "Whoever does the will of God is my brother and sister and mother" (Mark 3:35).

Verses 14-15. Paul's debt is the obligation he feels to share the good news with all classes of people in Roman society. These included the cultured (Greeks) and the uncultured (barbarians, those who spoke other languages and who were on the margins of Roman society), the highly educated (wise), and the slaves and working class who lacked the advantage of education (foolish).

Verses 16-17. Here Paul states the basic twofold purpose of his letter: to explain the gospel he plans to preach in both Rome and Spain when he gets there and to provide a basis for the unity of Jews and Gentiles in the church, that is, salvation by faith in Jesus Christ. The central themes of this message, developed later in the letter, are stated here as (1) the power of God, (2) salvation through faith, (3) the oneness of Jew and Gentile, and (4) the righteousness of God.

God is more powerful than the might of Rome. Thus Jew and Gentile alike may be saved by grace through faith in the death and resurrection of Christ. The life of righteousness through faith was known to the Jews, as the quotation from Habakkuk 2:4 in verse 17 reveals. But now this life is available to "everyone who has faith" (verse 16). No one need be ashamed of the good news. Everyone can claim it.

OUR NEED

◼ The writer's little brother mentioned in the student book [pages 6–7] knew instinctively that he could trust his father to catch him when he jumped from the porch. Confidence in a loving father inspired him to leap into that father's arms.

What do we put our trust in that might, like Dan's prankish brothers, let us down? Attractive appearance may fade with age. Wearing apparel goes out of style. Friends and family members may break their promises. Investments can drop in value. College degrees may not produce the job opportunities for which we had hoped. The family farm can be lost. Good health can vanish overnight. None of these or other "sure things" is fully reliable.

Only faith in God can save us. Only when we put our trust in the power and righteousness of God can we be assured that "things will turn out all right in the end." Paul's primary purpose for writing this letter to the Romans was precisely to explain the gospel of salvation through faith. "The one who is righteous will live by faith" (Romans 1:17).

Paul's other purpose was to establish a faith basis for the unity and reconciliation of Jew and Gentile in the Christian church. These parties were divided over a theological issue. Could persons be saved through faith in Christ alone, or must they observe the requirements and rituals of the law? Was righteousness a matter of right belief and right conduct or of trust in a gracious God and saving Lord alone?

Ask: **What questions of belief and conduct divide Christians today?** (Group members may mention the following: Is it ever right to get an abortion? If so, under what conditions? Should a person be permitted to take Communion before being baptized and joining the church? Should Christians practice civil disobedience when a law seems unjust? Is the Bible literally true? Can good people of other religions be saved?)

Ask: **How do you feel and behave toward people who disagree with you on these or other questions of faith?**

Are there some standards of belief and practice that, if violated, should put persons outside the faith community? (Pause for a minute, giving group members time to reflect.)

Continue: **Or should we accept persons as sisters and brothers in Christ regardless of what they believe?**

What is the basis for drawing the line between faith and unfaith? (Again, give group members time to reflect.)

Paul's answer in Romans is that all who accept "the power of God for salvation" (Romans 1:16) can become the righteous who "will live by faith" (Romans 1:17). All who trust God rather than the uncertain goods of human achievement or the guidelines of human codes and creeds are assured of redemption in Christ. To all these Paul says, "Grace to you and peace from God our Father and the Lord Jesus Christ" (Romans 1:7).

LESSON PLAN

◼ Drawing on the commentary above and the material in the student book [pages 5–13], lead the group in discussion, using the questions below.

(1) *What are some reasons that it was important to convince the Romans that faith is the only condition for salvation?*

Two crisis situations have been suggested as the occasion for Paul's writing. According to one interpretation, the house churches in Rome apparently were in disagreement over whether observance of the law was essential to salvation. The Jewish Christians or Judaizers took the traditional view. They, along with other Jews, had fled Rome under the persecution of the Emperor Claudius in A.D. 49 and now, after his death in 54, were returning and reopening their synagogues. But these people found that during their absence leadership had been taken by Gentile Christians who did not use the Jewish prayer book, hymns, calendar, and form of worship and did not adhere to Jewish ethical standards. In an effort to regain control of the churches, these Jewish Christians asserted that the Gentiles must accept and practice the ritual, dietary, and moral requirements of the law. Righteousness meant observance of the law. God blessed those who did the right thing.

The progressive position, that redemption in Christ freed Jew and Gentile alike from bondage to the law, was taken by the emerging Gentile Christian leadership who had remained behind. House churches representing the two camps were formed. The division separating the tiny Christian minority in the Empire's capital city was becoming a scandal. A strong message was desperately needed to convince both groups that neither rigid tradition nor undisciplined freedom was the way to salvation.

According to another interpretation, Paul was more concerned with his relationship to the Jewish Christians in Jerusalem. Advocates of this view cite Romans 15:30-33, verses that reveal Paul's concern regarding his upcoming visit to Jerusalem. Paul had collected money for the Christians there from his Gentile churches. The collection emphasized his understanding of the unity of the church of Jesus Christ. Absence of such unity would undermine the truth of the gospel as Paul had preached it: salvation for all through faith in Jesus Christ. Therefore, according to this understanding, Paul wrote to gain support both for his missionary efforts and for his vision of the one community united in faith.

Both interpretations center on the issue of faith and unity. Therefore they convey a common meaning for Christians today: The church is an inclusive community founded on saving faith in Jesus Christ.

(2) *When did you first become aware of justification (being saved) by faith?*

How did it affect you? (You may wish to ask group members to respond to this question, or you may want to witness to your own experience of salvation by faith.)

(3) *"What are some of your credentials for witnessing to the faith?"* [student book, page 10].

For some, a prior question may be, "What do I have to witness to and how do I go about it?" Discuss with the group how they represent their faith in Christ and his love in their homes, workplaces, neighborhoods, and communities. Possible forms of witness include upright living, honest dealings, inviting people to church, care of those in need, community service, working for change in unfair systems, telling our faith stories, and fair treatment of minorities.

The word *credentials* comes from the same root as "credence," "credibility," and "credo," which means "I believe" or "I set my heart." Thus our credentials are what make us believable or trustworthy.

Have the group share what they think makes them and their witness believable to those around them. Mention that an argument often made against attending church is that "too many Christians are hypocrites" or "Christians don't practice what they preach." This makes the same assumption that Paul was contending against in the Roman churches (and that I was raised with)—that being a "good Christian" means doing and believing the right things, obeying the rules, and staying out of trouble.

Ask: **Are these the credentials that make our witness believable?**

If so, what happens when we fail to live up to these standards?

Writing to people who had never met him, Paul asserts his claim to be a servant of Christ, called to be an apostle, set apart for the gospel, and a recipient of God's grace. Paul's credentials are not what good he has done but what Christ has done for him. The message he shares with the Romans is not, "Look at me and my accomplishments for Christ and follow my example." Rather, it is, "Look at Christ and his good news of salvation through grace."

(4) *"What kinds of things do you do to prepare for a discussion that may involve points of conflict?"* [student book, page 11].

Ask group members to recall a recent conflict or disagreement they experienced. Then ask a few people to share their experiences and how they handled them. List on a chalkboard or on a large sheet of paper ideas for effectively dealing with conflict that emerge out of members' experiences. Or list the following such guidelines:

(A) Listen carefully to what people are saying and tell them what you think you heard.

(B) Say clearly and directly what you think and feel.

(C) Assume the best about others. Do not attribute bad motives or intentions to them.

(D) Acknowledge your mistakes, and ask for forgiveness.

(E) Build up other people's self-esteem. Praise their strengths and assets. Help them feel good about themselves.

(F) Try to identify the key issue. What specifically do you disagree about? Keep the discussion focused on that.

(G) Think of as many possible solutions to the problem as possible. Do not limit the discussion to just two alternatives—yours and theirs. Find ideas or proposals that all can agree on and feel good about.

(H) Pray for one another. It is hard to think evil of others or to try to do them in when you are praying for them.

Paul practices some of these principles when he commends the faith of the Romans, anticipates mutual encouragement in his visit to them, and acknowledges his obligation to all types and classes of people.

(5) *"What are some of the insights about your faith that came to you through reading the Old Testament?"* [student book, page 12].

Look at Hebrews 11, which lists many Old Testament heroes and heroines of faith. Recall the faith stories of Abel, Noah, Abraham and Sarah, Isaac and Rebekah, Jacob and Rachel, Joseph, Moses and Miriam, Rahab, David, and others. Have the group name the qualities of faith exemplified by each. *(For example, Abel offered his best to God. Noah followed God's command. Abraham went out not knowing where he was to go. Rahab believed in God's power and so on.)*

(6) *"In what ways does faith prepare us to receive God's grace?"* [student book, page 13].

When John Wesley, founder of Methodism, was on a ship returning to England after failing as a missionary in Georgia, the Moravian Peter Böhler advised him to preach faith until he had it and after getting it, to preach faith because he had it. Wesley's mistake had been that he relied on good works and practical disciplines and not on faith in God's love—the same flaw that had plagued many Jewish Christians in the early church centuries before.

What Böhler was saying, and what Wesley finally realized when his "heart was strangely warmed" at Aldersgate, was that when we trust God for salvation and act as though we believe it even when we do not feel it, God's grace moves in our lives. God prepares us to launch out in faith even before we realize it. Wesley called this "prevenient grace" or grace that comes to us to prepare us for salvation.

Have group members tell of times when they launched out in faith when they could not predict the outcome. Ask: *When you look back on that now, can you see how God had prepared you for that step without your realizing it?*

Close the session by singing "My Faith Looks Up to Thee," followed by this litany:

Mention, one by one, experiences and insights class members have shared of becoming aware of justification by faith (Question 2), claiming their credentials for witnessing (Question 3), handling conflict effectively (Question 4), learning from the Old Testament (Question 5), and discovering grace and faith (Question 6). After mentioning each, ask the class to repeat this refrain: THANK YOU GOD, FOR YOUR GRACE.

Then pray in unison the prayer printed at the end of the lesson in the student book.

TRY ANOTHER METHOD

■ If the group is large or if time is limited, form six small groups and assign one of the questions above to each group. Have them write their responses on a chalkboard or on a large sheet of paper for reporting at the end of the session.

Ask the small group dealing with Question 1 to report in the form of a debate between the traditionalists and progressives in Rome about the way of salvation—faith versus works.

Group 2 might share how they discovered the meaning of justification by faith.

The third group could share their experiences of and feelings about witnessing and then tell what factors have made their witness of word or deed most believable.

Ask Group 4 to describe some of the conflict situations they have been involved in, how they handled them, and what guidelines for effective dealing with conflict they have discovered.

The small group discussing the question about faith in the Old Testament might read Hebrews 11, identify the faith qualities manifested by each of the characters mentioned there, and then discuss ways of expressing these qualities in our lives. This group could also look through the Old Testament for other examples and attributes of faith, such as the psalmist's trust in God, the denunciation of injustice by prophets like Amos and Jeremiah, the family loyalty of Ruth, the risk taken by Esther, and Isaiah's visions of God's holiness and peace.

The last small group could share experiences of risk-taking in the faith that God saw them through and then consider with the benefit of hindsight how God might have been sustaining them through those uncertain times.

Any of these approaches can also be used in the total group.

Chapter Two

RECEIVING GOD'S GIFT

PURPOSE

To help us recognize that in response to God's grace, faith in Christ has priority over obedience to the law

BIBLE PASSAGE

Romans 4:13-25
Background: Romans 3:21–4:25

CORE VERSE

The promise that he would inherit the world did not come to Abraham or to his descendants through the law but through the righteousness of faith. (Romans 4:13)

GET READY

■ Begin by praying for God's guidance in making this lesson applicable to the group members' spiritual and practical needs. Think over your common experiences with, attitudes toward, and understandings of various kinds of law.

Read the articles on "Abraham" and "law" in a good Bible dictionary. Also read the exposition of Romans 4:31-25 in a Bible commentary.

BIBLE BACKGROUND

■ The overall message of Romans 3:21–4:25 may be summarized as follows: The life, death, and resurrection of Jesus make possible our righteousness before God. Human sin and hostility against God were manifest in the Crucifixion, but we are forgiven through Christ's guiltless death. He died for us, that we might receive God's gift of grace.

The Resurrection confirmed the truth of God's revelation through Jesus Christ. In the light of Christ, we realize the barrenness of our former lives and are given the possibility of new life grounded in grace, not in human achievement.

God, who creates the universe, has also turned death into life. Our lives are sinful and empty, but God makes them good and full by the power of the Resurrection. Faith is trusting in this power of God in Christ. Abraham is the ancestor of all people of faith.

Romans 4:13. The word *for* refers to what Paul said in the preceding verses. The reason Abraham is the ancestor of all faithful people is that he acted by faith. The law is the law given to Moses, but God had made the promise to Abraham hundreds of years before the law came to Moses. God's "promise" is the sign of God's faithfulness, of which Paul is confident. The promise is to Abraham's offspring—in terms of faith, not of blood line. God would bless all families of the earth (Genesis 12:2-3) through the faith that Abraham first demonstrated. Abraham's faith was not, of course, in the promise as such but in the God who made it.

Verse 14. Here Paul contends with the legalists by setting law and promise in opposition to each other. He is not criticizing all those who keep the law but only those who make its observance central—those who trust, not in God, but in their human ability to follow rules and rituals. The law cannot be the way to God. If it were, then God's promise to Abraham would be empty; for Abraham was rewarded, not for works done, but for believing God and moving out in faith. The promise was not a reward for achievement but a free gift.

Verse 15. The law brings God's anger on us, for we are imperfect humans who cannot possibly keep all its provisions. And the law brings temptation to us: We try to get away with breaking the law, which then mandates punishment for our disobedience. But keeping the law will not bring salvation as a reward for virtue. Rather, it shows us our failings and our need for a savior. Without law there is no violation and hence no awareness of sin or necessity of salvation.

Verse 16. Because the law is ineffective as a path to God, only the promise of grace (God's free gift) can be trusted to provide salvation to all Abraham's heirs. These include both Jew ("adherents of the law") and Gentile ("those who share the faith of Abraham"). The two factions in the early church—and persons of all viewpoints in the church today—are united as children of a common ancestor and as recipients of a common gift.

Verse 17. Paul quotes Genesis 17:5 to show that God's covenant with Abraham is not racial, national, or religious but rather a matter of faith. God's power can bring life from death (meaning both Christ's resurrection and Sarah's conception of Isaac, as mentioned in verse 19). And out of nothing God's power can create the material universe, human beings in God's image, and a New Earth (Romans 8:18-25).

Verses 18-19. The rest of this passage joins Abraham's faith with hope and shows that these key qualities were expressed despite a realistic appraisal of the situation. The aged couple were deemed incapable of producing children. Yet because of their trust in God, the impossible happened; and a whole people—of both lineage and faith—was established. God considered such faith as righteousness, not only for them, but for all who have manifested faith from that day to this.

Hope, a word that Paul uses over a dozen times in Romans, carries a specific meaning. It rests in reliance on the character of God and hence is different from ordinary optimism. "Hoping against hope" means that Abraham believed God's promise even when there was no worldly evidence to support it. Ephesians 2:12 refers to people "having no hope and without God." The two go together: the presence of God and the presence of hope. Abraham and Sarah had both. As a result, they became parents "of many nations."

The word *Abram* means "exalted father." Today, Abraham is a patriarch to several Middle Eastern peoples and an important figure in three world religions: Judaism, Islam, and Christianity. His ancient journeys, launched in faithful response to God's direction, took him from Ur of the Chaldees (near Basra, on the border between present-day Iran and Iraq), to Haran (in southern Turkey just north of Syria), and then to Shechem (in present-day Israel). Thus he traversed much of the Near East, and his memory is revered throughout that region. Although Paul alludes to this regional importance with his quotation from Genesis, he is clear that Abraham's significance for Christians lies in the patriarch's faith and hope.

Verse 20. Despite their advanced age, Abraham and Sarah did not waver in their faith in God's promise to give them a child. It was God, not their faith in itself, that made them strong. We are not saved by faith but by grace through faith. When God's promise was fulfilled, Abraham and Sarah gave God the credit for what was happening (unlike the sinners mentioned in Romans 1:21, who "though they knew God, they did not honor him as God or give thanks to him"). Abraham and Sarah recognized God's glory and acknowledged themselves as creatures in relation to their Creator.

Verse 21. Actually, Abraham laughed when he heard that Sarah would conceive (Genesis 17:17-18), which suggests that he may not always have been "fully convinced." He knew that, humanly speaking, the likelihood of such an older couple having a baby was laughable, whereas with "God all things are possible" (Matthew 19:26). It was a long time between when the promise was given (Genesis 13:16) and when it was fulfilled (Genesis 21:2); but the faith of Abraham and Sarah, though severely tested, held firm.

Verse 22. It was this steadiness of faith that God reckoned as righteousness. Here, as in verse 3, Paul is quoting from Genesis 15:6.

Verses 23-25. In concluding this passage, Paul relates salvation by faith to Christ's death and resurrection. The first Christians' experience of salvation was like that of a new creation. Their old life and world were done away with, and a new self and lifestyle were brought into being. Through God's grace they could admit that their former lives had been empty and sinful, but God through Christ had given them new life and hope. As Jesus died and was raised, so God can change our lives from void to fullness. Christ died to show us the extent to which God would go to offer us forgiveness. And he was raised to demonstrate that

God has the power to justify us (to credit us as righteous) in spite of our sin. Our ability to live a holy life does not rest, therefore, in observance of codes of laws or codes of ethics but in the strength given by God for a resurrected, transformed life in Christ's love.

OUR NEED

■ Share the following story with the group:

As a teenager Sally Steele (not her real name) felt unloved, unaccepted, and pressured to please her parents. As a result, she developed anorexia nervosa and was slowly starving herself to death. Her mother took her to Sunday school and brought her up to avoid the wrong and to live by high moral standards. "I had a desire in my heart to be good," Sally told me; "but I didn't know the Lord." In high school she had an inferiority complex, began to hate herself, felt lonely and unloved, and "really wanted to die. I didn't have anyone to just hold me and say you're OK as a person." When she went off to college, she was quickly disillusioned by the morals of her classmates. "It just blew my little world all to pieces. Other people didn't share my moral standards. I had been living in a make-believe world. I didn't want to go to college, really; I was there to please my father."

And then "the Lord led into my life the man who is now my husband." It was his strong, steadfast love that began to convince Sally of her own self-worth. "He was the one that the Lord used to show me that I could be loved unconditionally. I would get hateful because I wanted people to love me, but he was always there. Whether I did the right things or the wrong things, he always loved me. He was the first person I ever knew who was Christlike."

He was back home; and she was at college, lonely and confused. When she came home for a weekend, he told her, "If you would ask, the Lord would answer; if you would knock, he would open the door; and if you'd seek, you would receive."

So Sally went back to the Wesley Fellowship on campus and attended a Wednesday night Communion service. "I was kneeling there and feeling so terrible; and the Lord Jesus was saying, 'If you just give it up, I'll take it over.' At that point I *knew* Jesus was Lord; I *knew* he could carry all these things that were about to crush me. So I gave my heart to him and understood that he really came for *me*. That was when my life began to change, when I began to understand that Christianity was more than just going to church and being a good person. I wanted to die physically, but I died to what I wanted and let him come into my heart."

Sally had been taught that to be a good Christian meant to "keep the law" of church attendance and right conduct. Religion for her was a matter of moralism and respectability. She was burdened with the compulsion to meet her parents' expectations and with the guilt of falling short. Human efforts at being good could not save her; in fact, they were destroying her.

Sally was saved when a loving human being who accepted her as she was introduced her to a loving God who also accepted her and gave her the gift of grace at a Communion altar. The body broken and the cup poured out spoke to her of Jesus Christ's death and resurrection, and she *knew* that he had died for her. Sally is one of the descendants of Abraham and Sarah who received the promise that they "would inherit the world . . . not . . . through the law but through the righteousness of faith" (Romans 4:13).

LESSON PLAN

■ Drawing on the commentary above and the material in the student book [pages 14–21], lead the group in discussion using the questions below.

(1) *"In what ways do you find God revealed in the Old Testament?*

"What additional insights does the New Testament bring to your understanding?" [student book; page 17].

Following Paul, the writer of the student book links Christian faith in God to Abraham's faith, though pointing out Paul's differences with the Hebrew tradition. In both the Old and the New Testament, God is described as being almighty, holy, loving, ever-present, righteous, all-knowing, faithful, creating, approachable, delivering, ruling, forgiving, generous, angry, glorious, great, jealous, judging, impartial, infinite, majestic, kind, merciful, protecting, nearby, perfect, redeeming, sovereign, wise, sustaining, unchanging, and wonderful.

Old Testament instances when people meet God in one or more of these dimensions include the command to Noah to build the ark (Genesis 6), Jacob's dream (Genesis 28), Jacob's encounter with the angel (Genesis 32), Joseph's dreams (Genesis 37), Moses' call (Exodus 3), Moses' receiving the Ten Commandments (Exodus 19), Joshua's vision at Jericho (Joshua 5), Ruth's promise to Naomi (Ruth 1), Hannah's prayer (1 Samuel 1–2), Samuel's call (1 Samuel 3), David's anointing (1 Samuel 16), Ezra's prayer (Ezra 9), Job's encounter with the Creator (Job 38–42), David's prayer of penitence (Psalm 51), the psalmist's prayers of faith and hope, Isaiah's vision (Isaiah 6), Jeremiah's call (Jeremiah 1), God's demand for justice (Amos 5:21-24 and Micah 6:8), and God's expression of compassion in Hosea (11:1-9).

Jesus revealed this God in his teaching; in his ministry; and in his own life, death, and resurrection. Paul's teaching about God in the Letter to the Romans is consistent with the Old Testament. However, Paul focuses on God's gift of grace and salvation through the death and resurrection of Jesus Christ.

(2) *"How does the realization that all believers are of one ancestry affect your appreciation of other members of the wider community of faith?"* [student book; page 18].

This question refers to Paul's assertion that all persons of faith are descendants of Abraham, whose faith God saw as righteousness. Paul made a similar point in his sermon in Athens: "The God who made the world and everything in it . . . from one ancestor . . . made all nations to inhabit the whole earth" (Acts 17:24-26). Paul here names Adam and Eve rather than Abraham and Sarah as ancestors of the whole human family, but the effect is the same. All human beings belong to one another because we are God's children, issuing from the first parents who were created by God; and we are invited to accept God's gift of righteousness through the first faith parents, Abraham and Sarah.

Ask the group how this fact might influence their attitudes toward persons of another race, social class, nation, religion, or doctrinal belief. Give substance to the questions by using the following examples: a new neighbor who is of another race, a homeless person living on the streets, an AIDS victim, a famine victim, a Muslim student attending a nearby college, a charismatic Christian.

Ask: *Are these persons our brothers and sisters?*
If so, in what respect?
How are we like them?
How are we different?
How should Christians treat them?

(3) *What similarities are there between some of the expectations in today's churches and the legalism of the Hebrew law?*
How do these affect you?
When we think of law, we could mention several kinds: the law of the land; the law of human nature; and the law of a religious community, for example. In Paul's time, the law of the land was the Roman law, which kept people in line; and the law of the religious community was the Hebrew Torah, which showed the way to get right with God. The law of human nature, which Paul discusses in Romans 7, is our self-centeredness, the source of human sin.

Ask the group for examples of all three types of law. Traffic, estate, and criminal laws would illustrate the law of the land. The urge to push to the head of the line, to spend money on oneself, to move up to a bigger house or car, to advertise to sell more regardless of what people need, and to maximize immediate profits at the expense of polluting the environment are examples of the inner law of human greed. Moral codes for everything from dress and etiquette to sexual and family relationships as a basis for acceptability for church membership correspond to the Jewish law in Paul's time.

Tell group members you are going to pose a series of questions for personal reflection. Then ask: *How does each type of law affect you?*
Do you obey the law of the land out of fear, out of duty, or out of respect?
Or do you try to get away with evading it?
How is self-centeredness expressed in your life, and how do you try to overcome it?
What tests for acceptability operate in our church?
Whom do we accept or reject and for what reasons?
How do we treat people who violate our standards of behavior?

(4) *"What questions do you have about physical and moral law? How does God help you cope with your questions?"* [student book; page 20].

In the student book section entitled "Law and Grace," laws of the universe and the moral life are mentioned. The former include the laws of gravity and the conservation of energy; the latter include the Ten Commandments. Both laws have definite and predictable consequences when a person attempts to break them. Jumping from heights breaks bodies. Lying and stealing break relationships. Polluting rivers kills fish. Dishonoring parents or children kills a family.

What is puzzling, however, is that sometimes people can break these laws and (apparently) get away with it. A child is killed in an auto accident, and the drunk driver who caused it escapes unharmed. A polluting company pays a bribe; or a government conceals the effects of nuclear radiation, and unborn babies appear with birth defects. The advertiser gets rich, and the wage earner is saddled with credit card debts. A person has a secret affair, and the unsuspecting spouse goes on loving him or her. Domestic abuse goes undetected, and children carry the scars into adult life.

Our freedom from the law does *not* free us from responsibility with respect to either laws of the universe or laws of the moral life. We know what we have done and whom we have hurt, and we will carry the guilt with us until we confess our sin to God and seek forgiveness. The harm we have done cannot be undone; but our sin can be forgiven, and relationships can be healed. Paul's message is that, through faith, the grace of a loving God conquers our sin, forgives our guilt, reckons us as righteous, and restores our broken relationships. Thanks be to God!

(5) *"How does Paul's message of salvation by grace help you in your efforts to bring the love of Christ to people in our time?"* [student book; page 21].

The lesson in the student book poses this question after showing how Paul's explanation of salvation by grace was helpful to both Jew and Gentile in the Roman churches and in other churches during the early years of the Christian movement.

Ask group members to recall times when people have come to them with questions about the faith or with problems in relationships with family, friends, the church, or God. Say: *How did you respond?*

How did you help, or how do you wish you had helped?

How did your understanding of grace influence the way you handled the situation?

How might you have handled things differently?

How does the idea of salvation by grace strengthen your own spiritual life?

You may ask group members to speak to these questions, or you may have them reflect in silence for two or three minutes. Either way, help group members understand that the God who calls us to these opportunities also promises to grant us wisdom to deal with them, to accept and bless our efforts, to forgive our failures, and to make "all things work together for good for those who love God, who are called according to his purpose" (Romans 8:28).

To close the session, have group members sing the hymn "Amazing Grace." Then lead the group in the prayer printed at the end of the lesson in the student book.

TRY ANOTHER METHOD

■ Ask several group members to look up and read some of the Old Testament passages mentioned in Question 1. After each reading, have the group identify the characteristics of God revealed in the passage.

Ask for three volunteers, one to represent the law of the land, one the law of human nature, and one the law of a religious community (Question 3). Pick one or more examples of questionable moral behavior—such as speeding, false advertising, sexual harassment, or spreading rumors about a church member—and have the three comment on the behavior from the perspective each represents.

In regard to each of the examples of breaking physical and moral laws mentioned in Question 4, ask: *How can we encourage people to accept responsibility for their conduct?*

Which is more effective, tougher laws with stiffer penalties or better opportunities for education and personal development that foster people's self-esteem and self-discipline?

How can we help people find God's forgiveness and healing for their sin and their broken relationships?

For Question 5, have a few group members roleplay a situation in which someone comes for help with a faith question or with a relationship problem—such as how God answers prayer or whether every word in the Bible is literally true or how to deal with a rebellious teenager. Then lead the entire group in a discussion of how the roleplay volunteers handled the situation, asking for suggestions regarding other approaches that might be used.

To end the session, have the group members join hands in a circle to sing "Amazing Grace." Then invite each person to turn to the group member on either side and say, "You are forgiven." Finally, pray the closing prayer from the student book.

Chapter Three

BEING RECONCILED TO GOD

PURPOSE

To help increase our understanding of the meaning of justification and reconciliation in Christ

BIBLE PASSAGE

Romans 5:6-17
Background: Romans 5

CORE VERSE

God proves his love for us in that while we still were sinners Christ died for us. (Romans 5:8)

GET READY

■ During the week pray for your group members, asking God to prepare their hearts for participation in the coming session.

Read the exposition of Romans 5 in a commentary and articles on "Justification" and "Reconciliation" in a Bible dictionary or a word book such as the one by Alan Richardson, mentioned in the lesson in the student book.

Be prepared to share an experience in which you were reconciled to God, to another person, or to yourself. Our gospel is grounded in the incarnation of Jesus Christ, the Word made flesh; a concrete human story is often the best way of making the meaning of the gospel clear.

BIBLE BACKGROUND

■ Romans 5:1-11 introduces the key themes of Chapters 5–8. In spite of present sufferings, the peace we find in being reconciled to God brings assurance of our salvation, both present and future. This peaceful relationship with God and with other persons, which comes through Jesus Christ's death and resurrection, is all the more wonderful in that it is given in a world ruled by evil powers. Our suffering at their hands builds character and deepens the hope grounded in God's love.

The central ideas in this passage are justification and reconciliation. Justification by faith sets right our status before God by canceling our sin through trust in Jesus Christ's death and resurrection. Our sins are forgiven, and God views and treats us as righteous. In reconciliation, the broken relationships between human beings and God, other persons, and the self are restored. Trust and harmony prevail anew. Justification makes sinners righteous; reconciliation restores severed relationships.

Romans 5:6. Christ's death was for sinners, for us. We were weak in our capacity to do right, to understand godly things, and to help ourselves out of our predicament. But God's love, shown on the cross, succeeds where human strength fails. Christ came at just the right time, fulfilling God's plan and meeting our need.

Verse 7. Few people have the courage to sacrifice their lives for others. Once in a while, we hear of one who enters an icy stream or a burning building to rescue someone from sure death. Dietrich Bonhoeffer; Martin Luther King, Jr.; Archbishop Oscar Romero; and the nuns martyred in El Salvador and Liberia are reverently remembered for giving their lives in the cause of justice and love for the poor and oppressed. Most of us are never put in a position to test our courage in this way. Could we choose to die for what we believe in or to save another? Jesus is the premiere instance of one who, filled with God's Spirit, gives his life for others. Indeed, Jesus died to save all humankind.

Verse 8. Paul says that through the cross God proves the lengths to which love will go to bring us back into right relationships with God, others, and ourselves. On the face of it, we might think that the cross shows just the opposite: An indifferent God allows an evil system and those who use it for their own selfish ends to destroy a good and innocent person. Through the centuries, both before and after Jesus, countless people in desperate situations have cried out to God, "Why, oh why, did you allow this to happen?" But Paul explains that Jesus' death is actually an expression of divine love, not divine disregard; for "in Christ God was reconciling the world to himself" (2 Corinthians 5:19). In Christ the sacrificial deaths of others gain meaning and purpose as well, for no sparrow falls without God's knowledge (Matthew 10:29); and God's purposes of hope and new life are served when any "grain of wheat falls into the earth and dies" (John 12:24). It is a basic principle of life that suffering, though never pleasant and sometimes inflicted with evil intent, can be redemptive when chosen for a greater good, endured bravely, and healed by God's grace. God overcomes evil through sacrificial love.

Christ's sacrifice was for those still in the state of sin—not for the worthy, but the unworthy. God loves because of who God is, not because of who we are. Awe and gratitude for the greatness of this sacrificial gift make up our appropriate response.

Verse 9. Paul is confident that, as Christ's death has restored us to God's favor, we will also be spared the effects of God's anger, which sinners justly deserve. The future tense ("will be saved") indicates that Paul is referring to the Last Judgment. Justification is effected by God's grace (Romans 3:24) and received by our faith (3:28). We participate in the life of the risen Lord (4:25) and are accepted by God (8:33) in the name of the Lord Jesus Christ and in the Spirit of God (1 Corinthians 6:11). These are all aspects of God's saving act in Christ.

Verse 10. Because the Crucifixion has brought about our reconciliation to God in spite of our hostility, it is certain that the Resurrection will save us for eternity.

Verse 11. We rejoice that in Christ our relationship with God has been restored. This reconciliation provides a basis for coping with whatever problems this evil world may give us.

Verse 12. Here Paul introduces a section that discusses some controversial themes—how sin originated and how Christ's kingdom is related to the sinful world (Adam). The assumption here, consistent with Jewish thinking in those times, is that sin entered the world through Adam and Eve, whose actions determined the fate of the whole human race. But the final clause states the opposite, that "all have sinned" and hence all persons must take responsibility for their actions. As descendants of Adam and Eve, we share in the sin of the entire human race; but we also are held individually accountable for our deeds. Original sin comes in part from the fact that we are born into a sinful world, but we ourselves also perpetuate sin. Paul here holds in tension the deterministic and the voluntary notions of sin. As sin entered the world through Adam, so did death—physical death, to be sure, but also spiritual death, the ultimate separation of human beings from God.

Verses 13-14. The account of the Fall in Genesis 3:1-19 is the background for Paul's observation that, while sin entered the world before the law given to Moses, it is the law that both makes us aware of our sinful inclination and provides us with a standard for judging sin. While Paul viewed Adam as a historical figure, here he refers to him as a type or pattern of the sinful human tendency to want to be like God. But the human situation was not to be determined by self-centeredness; "the one who was to come" would overcome evil with good.

Verses 15-17. Here Paul contrasts the impact of Adam (sin) and Christ (grace) in terms of:

—death of many vs. free gift in grace for many
—condemnation vs. justification
—trespass vs. righteousness
—dominion of death vs. dominion in life

The new era, characterized by grace, life, acquittal, obedience, and righteousness, is engaged in mortal combat with the old era of condemnation, death, judgment, disobedience, and sin. Each has its followers, and those who serve Christ will suffer for their faith. But the outcome is assured. Grace will conquer sin. Christ's domain is greater than Adam's. The bottom line is a word of hope and assurance. This is the message Paul shares with the Roman Christians and hopes to carry to the people of Spain.

OUR NEED

■ Kaye was facing another crisis in her family. A forty-nine-year-old widow who had already weathered the premature death of her husband, she was now confronted with a police report indicating that Jim, her teenage son, had been caught shoplifting. She had been concerned for some time about the company Jim was keeping, and she suspected that he was taking drugs. Now she would have to accompany him to court while dealing with her own sense of failure as a parent.

She had felt the growing strain between them in recent months and had responded with scolding and pressure to try to get Jim to shape up. He in turn had become increasingly sullen and resentful, and at this point they were barely speaking.

The previous month a group of parents had met in her home to discuss the growing drug problem in the high school. The consultant they had invited was a young man who had been cured of his drug addiction by accepting Jesus Christ. His parting words that night, "Have you tried God?" had made a strong impression. They had led her back to the church and faith of her youth; and last Sunday in the adult Bible class she had been deeply touched by a passage from Hosea:

> When Israel was a child, I loved him,
>   and out of Egypt I called my son.
> The more I called them,
>   the more they went from me;
> they kept sacrificing to the Baals,
>   and offering incense to idols.
>
> Yet it was I who taught Ephraim to walk,
>   I took them up in my arms;
>   but they did not know that I healed them.
> I led them with cords of human kindness,
>   with bands of love.
>
>   (Hosea 11:1-4)

What struck her was the similarity between God's grief over Israel's waywardness and her own feelings toward Jim. She had raised him from infancy, had supported him in the loss of his father, and had tried to be both father and mother to him; but now all she was getting was defiance. Yet what also impressed her was that God still loved those willful children of Israel. She was berating Jim, but God led Israel "with cords of human kindness." Was she being too hard on her son? Maybe she should just accept him as he is and try loving him in his rebellion.

Over the next several months Kaye bit her lip, returned insults with kindness, went with him to court, stood by him while he was on probation, and prayed for him daily. Gradually, their relationship began to change. Jim's dark moods began to lighten. He told his mother where he was going. Different friends appeared at the door. His grades started to improve. They had brief conversations at the breakfast table. He even offered to go to church with her.

Kaye and Jim's relationship was not out of the woods yet when I talked with her. But much healing had taken place. By changing her attitude from condemnation to forgiveness, she offered Jim grace. Accepting him as he was was a kind of justification (reckoning as righteous). Her return to the church and faith was a kind of resurrection or new birth that had brought reconciliation not only with God but also with her son. Being "justified by faith," she had found "peace with God"—and her son, Jim—"through our Lord Jesus Christ" (Romans 5:1).

LESSON PLAN

■ Ask the group what they understand by the key words *justification* and *reconciliation*. Summarize the explanations given above and in the student book. Then, drawing on the commentary above and the material in the student book [pages 22–30], lead the group in discussion using the questions below.

(1) *"How have you experienced peace and glory in your Christian life?"* [student book; page 25].

In the student book a discussion of the results of justification by faith—peace with God, contentment of spirit, assurance of God's love, the joy of salvation, and the hope of glory both now and in the life to come—precedes this question. These are magnificent benefits but need to be illustrated in life experience.

Ask the group members to share their experiences of being reconciled to another person or to God. Begin by telling your own story or this one of mine:

Some time ago I felt a friend had deeply wronged me. I felt he owed me an apology; but each time I saw him, he acted as though nothing had happened. I did not confront him but began avoiding him, held a grudge, and "wrote him off my list." I was harboring a hurt and a hate.

Then one time in an informal worship service we were asked to mill around and say to those we met, "You are forgiven." I tried to stay away from him; but as luck (or God!) would have it, I found him right in front of me. Not knowing what else to do, I looked him in the eye and said the prescribed words: "You are forgiven." My heart was not really in it, but the Spirit of God worked the miracle anyway.

Almost at once a glorious feeling of deep peace came into my heart. The load of hurt and hate was lifted, and we were friends again. He had not acknowledged the wrong, but God had given me the strength to forgive him anyway. Our relationship has been improving ever since. By the grace of God—certainly not through any good intention on my part—we have been reconciled! And the sense of peace and glory continues to abide.

(2) *"What are the true objectives of Christian hope? How do we reach them?"* [student book; page 26].

This question grows out of the comments in the student book on the following passage: "We also boast in our sufferings, knowing that suffering produces endurance, and endurance produces character, and character produces hope, and hope does not disappoint us, because God's love has been poured into our hearts through the Holy Spirit that has been given to us" (Romans 5:3-5).

Clarence Jordan paraphrases these verses as, "We also get 'status' for getting banged up, being fully aware that getting banged up makes us tough. Now toughness makes for reliability and reliability for confidence, and confidence doesn't let you down. For God has given us a love transfusion by the Holy Spirit he provided for us."[1]

What Jordan refers to as reliability Paul calls character, which the student book defines as "the inner moral strength that underlies hope" [pages 25–26]. The personal qualities mentioned in this passage are the true objective of hope.

You may wish to share the following story and comments with your group:

While visiting the church in Chengdu, China, I met a venerable pastor named Daniel Li Lian Ke, then eighty-seven. He had come to West China in 1940 as a refugee, then stayed there during the war with Japan. He was imprisoned for several years during the Cultural Revolution when all churches were closed. Some of the church buildings were used as warehouses, and others were torn down. While in jail he was kept in a cell with nine others; but he told me, "I was protected; it was those on the outside who received the cruel treatment." He admitted, however, that "the reason I cannot walk well today is because there was no heat in the prison, and we slept on the floor."

When I met him, Daniel Li was the leader of the Christians of Chengdu—chief pastor of the church; principal of the seminary; a saintly, kindly, gentle man who had earned the respect of Christian and non-Christian alike because of his courage in witnessing for his faith in the midst of suffering.

We attended a packed service with 700 worshipers—only one of several services that Sunday—in which over 100 new Christians were baptized. When I asked Mr. Li to explain the amazing recent growth of the church in China, he had two answers: the work of the Holy Spirit and the people's growing realization that "there is more to life than what they can see and touch, that they must live for something higher. The Christian gospel is the only thing in China pointing to that something higher." But there is a third reason: the life and witness through suffering—the character and hope—of saints like Daniel Li Lian Ke.

(3) *Are you comfortable with Paul's understanding of justification by faith? Why or why not?*

If not, what would you change?

The lesson in the student book contrasts the Christian message of salvation through God's free grace with the psychological concepts of positive and negative reinforcement, reward and punishment. "We are forgiven because God loves us, not because we have done anything to deserve it" [student book; page 27].

Recall the story in the student book of the neighbors who were reconciled and the story of Kaye and her son, Jim, in this teacher book. With regard to each, ask: **Which was or would have been most effective in this situation: negative reinforcement (punishment), positive reinforcement (reward), or grace?**

Now call out the following list of criminals, crimes, and offenses: bank robber, serial killer, arsonist, rapist, adulterer, terrorist, a crime reported in last week's news, a gang-related killing, discharging poisonous wastes into the environment, depriving the sick of needed health care, foreclosing on a mortgage and evicting folks from their family farm, the genocide of six million Jews in gas ovens. After each one ask: **Does God love this person?** or **Would God forgive the person who did this?**

Then ask: **Does God put conditions on forgiveness?**
If so, what are they?
If not, what restraints are there on human behavior?
What is the relation between repentance and forgiveness?
What experience have you had with either giving or receiving unconditional acceptance?

Remind the group of the definitions of justification (being viewed as righteous) and reconciliation (healing of relationships) given above. Repeat the Key Verse in unison. Then ask: *What does this mean for the persons committing the offenses just discussed?*

(4) *Can you remember times when someone's love made you a better person?*

Can you remember times when your love made someone else a better person?

If so, what were the circumstances?

Examples here could be the love of a spouse or parent, a congregation's support of persons newly divorced, giving a job to a paroled convict, asking forgiveness for deceiving someone, being forgiven for slighting another. If the group members are slow to respond, refer to my illustration of saying "You are forgiven" to the friend who had hurt me. With regard to each story mentioned by group members, ask: *What were the obstacles to expressing love and forgiveness?*

How were they overcome?

How did the person feel who was forgiving? the person who was forgiven?

How was each made a better person?

What part did God play?

(5) *When have you found reconciliation with God? with yourself?*

Ask members to share stories of their conversion to Christ or of times when they have felt distant from God or out of sorts with themselves and then found inner healing through prayer. Begin with an example from your own life. Such instances as restored faith in oneself after the loss of a job, new meaning found through disillusionment, being saved during adolescence, gaining a new sense of purpose after the empty nest or retirement, or being lifted from depression by an inspiring worship service might be mentioned. As each

is shared, ask: *What part did faith and grace play in this? What was God saying or doing in this experience?*

Close the session by having the group sing "Help Us Accept Each Other." Then offer a prayer of thanksgiving for the experiences of reconciliation that have been shared and for God's grace that has made these experiences of reconciliation possible.

[1]From *The Cotton Patch Version of Paul's Epistles,* by Clarence Jordan (Association Press, 1968); page 23.

TRY ANOTHER METHOD

■ Form teams of two persons. Then assign one or more verses from Romans 5:6-17 to each team, asking them to paraphrase the verses in their own words. Read aloud Jordan's paraphrase of Romans 5:3-5 as an example. Ask the teams to discuss these questions:

What changes in my life would be required if I really took this seriously?

What changes would we need to make in our church?

What changes would take place in the world if people lived by these verses?

Then invite the members to share their paraphrases and their responses to the questions with the total group. Compare their paraphrases with the commentary on these verses in the "Hearing the Word" section above.

List the suggested changes on a chalkboard or on a large sheet of paper in three columns: "Self," "Church," and "World." Invite the group to add to the list.

In a spirit of prayer read the items aloud one by one, asking the group to respond after each with the words, "Spirit of God, empower us to make this change."

Chapter Four

DELIVERED FROM SIN

PURPOSE

To help us consider how God's grace frees us to say no to old ways and yes to new life in Christ

BIBLE PASSAGE

Romans 6:3-14, 20-23
Background: Romans 6

> ### CORE VERSE
> For the wages of sin is death, but the free gift of God is eternal life in Christ Jesus our Lord.
> (Romans 6:23)

GET READY

■ Pray for God's guidance as you prepare to lead the group and for the receptivity and openness of group members to participate and grow in their Christian faith and life.

Read the exposition of Romans 6 in a Bible commentary and articles on "Sin" and "Sanctification" in a Bible dictionary or word book.

Think through and write out your own definitions of *sin* and *sanctification*. Be prepared to share a memory of a meaningful baptism experience—yours or someone else's.

BIBLE BACKGROUND

■ The three sections of Romans 6 are verses 1-14, Sin and Baptism; 15-19, Sin and Lordship; and 20-23, Sanctification. The chapter raises some major doctrinal issues that have troubled the church ever since the letter was written, such as, Can Christians sin after being saved (perfectionism and sanctification)? What is the significance of baptism for the Christian life? and, What is meant by union with Christ (mysticism)?

The chapter begins by noting the inconsistency of a Christian living in sin when sin has been conquered through Christ's death and resurrection. Paul next explains that this contradiction is overcome in baptism in which entering the water represents dying to sin and rising out of the water symbolizes freedom to begin a new life in Christ. Verse 14 concludes that sin can no longer rule the believer, who lives under grace, not under law. Salvation replaces slavery to sin with obedience to the new Lord of righteousness. The result of the former was death, while the benefits of the new servanthood are holiness and eternal life.

Romans 6:1-2. Here Paul poses a key question for the Christian faith: Is there any real difference between life in the old era and life in the new? Does sin still control the world? The conduct of Christians, such as the ugly infighting between traditionalists and progressives in the Roman churches, makes one wonder if anything has really changed. Paul is challenging his readers, then and now: If you have in fact died to sin, why are you still living in it? What good have Christ's death and resurrection really done if you in the church are still living like those in the world? Even though sin is often found in the church, it does not have to be that way. Your sinful ways are an embarrassing contradiction to God's gift of new life in Christ.

Verses 3-7. An experience common to all Christians—baptism—is here used to emphasize the inconsistency of Christians living in sin when they have received grace. The Romans to whom Paul was writing had likely been baptized in response to believing the gospel. Early Christian baptism was a dramatic occasion. After months of instruction, on Easter eve the catechumens [kat-ih-KYOO-muhns]—new converts in training—separated into groups of men and women and took the sacred vows before the congregation. The catechumens then disrobed, entered the baptismal pool, were anointed with oil, and were submerged in the water in the name of Father, Son, and Spirit. They then rose from the water, donned white robes symbolizing cleansing and new life, and received welcome into the community as full members.

Several years ago I stood in a baptistry in the ruins of an ancient church in Emwas, Israel—a supposed site of the biblical town of Emmaus. As I took the three steps down into the baptistry, I imagined myself in the Greco-Roman society of the third century: The surrounding culture is alien to the Christian faith, and yet I am led to join the Christians and become baptized. I enter the baptistry, then rise, dripping wet, a new creature in Christ Jesus. With the white baptismal robe I put on a new identity and take my place in a hostile world as a member of the new movement.

I have joined a group of people who are being persecuted for turning the world upside down. Through our baptism we have said no to the ways of sin and death. We have set out to change the sinful structures and relationships of our society in order that they might follow the laws of love and justice. In our baptism we have committed our lives to leading the world out of the old era into the new. We have taken on the identity of followers of Christ and have assumed a new lifestyle, which chooses giving over getting, serving over being served, and sharing over hoarding.

To be baptized as a Christian means the same in the twenty-first century as it did in the first. We die to the old and rise to the new. We have joined a movement dedicated to overcoming slavery to sin and transforming the world according to the image of Jesus Christ.

Verse 3 speaks of being baptized "into his death," which means that Christ took upon himself a death that we deserved. In baptism we identify with Christ's death by decisively turning our backs on the old life of sin. Verse 4 makes this even more emphatic by using the word *buried*. The phrase "united with him" in verse 5 points to the fact that it is only through being identified with Christ's death to conquer sin that we can be raised with him to new life. "Our old self was crucified with him" (verse 6), which brings freedom from slavery to sin (verse 7).

Verses 8-11. The theme of dying to the old and rising to the new in Christ continues here. As Christ died to sin and lives to God, so can we. Our new relationship with God through Christ empowers us to turn our backs on a life of sin and self-centeredness and to begin a new life in God. The reign of sin over us has been broken, and we are born into a new life in Christ.

The words *no longer* in verse 9 suggest that while Christ suffered on earth, death had dominion over him because he submitted to it (Philippians 2:7-8). But this is no longer the case; for in the Resurrection, Christ has conquered death once and for all. For this reason we also must view ourselves as "dead to [rejecting] sin and alive to [accepting] God in Christ Jesus" (verse 11).

The being united with Christ in death and resurrection (verse 5) and the "in Christ" here likely do not refer to a self merged with God in mystical union. Rather, they point to an identification with Christ through prayer and commitment to die to the old and rise to the new. While Paul does have a close personal relationship with Christ and proclaims this possibility to all, his is not the classical form of mysticism that loses touch with time and space. Rather, for Paul the believer continues to live in the historical realm between Christ's death and resurrection in the past and the coming resurrection and final victory in the future.

Our relationship with Christ is not one of union or fusion but rather is more like a "marriage, a relationship in which Christ remains Lord and in which the believer remains the servant."[1] We have become tied to our Savior; we have ceased being "in ourselves" in order to be "in him." Only as we are "in Christ" can we live "to God."

Verses 12-14. The new relationship with Christ must lead to a new way of life in which our bodies no longer serve as "instruments of wickedness" but are offered to God as "instruments of righteousness." The contradiction between having been saved by grace and still living in sin can continue no longer. Ethical living must flow from our new saving relationship with Christ. The tendency to sin, which controlled us, must do so no longer; for we are "not under law but under grace." Paul calls us to live transformed lives, to become what we now are. "So if anyone is in Christ, there is a new creation: everything old has passed away; see, everything has become new!" (2 Corinthians 5:17).

Verses 20-23. The third section of this chapter discusses sanctification. There was no benefit to living in sin; it led only to death. But the gain in serving God is sanctification (holiness); it leads to everlasting life. God's grace in Christ not only justifies us, that is, changes our status before God from being viewed as sinful to being viewed as righteous. It also sanctifies us, that is, makes us holy. We are empowered to lead changed lives—good, moral, offered to God. Both are gifts of God through Christ's death and resurrection. This is not, however, a magical change that makes leading a holy life effortless and easy. Having been "freed from sin" (verse 22), we now must develop the gift by committing ourselves to God's service. One definition of sanctify is "to set apart to a sacred purpose or to religious use." As sanctified persons we are called to devote ourselves to the ways of God. This involves prayer, worship, Bible study, personal morality, and responsible living in the world. Holiness is both a divine gift and a human responsibility.

John Wesley, founder of Methodism, spoke of sanctification in terms of "Christian perfection" and "growing in grace." Although Christians do make bad choices after being justified, we must repent of such choices and strive to do "good works" if we "expect to be made perfect in this life." These good works include both service to God (the "holy habits" of religious discipline) and "works of charity" (mercy) to meet the needs of our neighbors. Jesus' Great Commandment (Mark 12:28-31) calls us to love both God and neighbor. Therefore commitment to God requires both acts of devotion and deeds of service. For Paul "the wages of sin is death, but the free gift of God is eternal life in Christ Jesus our Lord" (verse 23). Our response to this good news of salvation must be to live holy (dedicated to God) and righteous (ethical) lives.

OUR NEED

■ Some time ago in our congregation a young woman whom I shall call Jane was baptized. She and her husband had been an intellectual, agnostic, young couple with no room for faith in their lives. They wanted to be good parents and, initially, came to our church at the urging of their children. But something about the quality of life in our congregation appealed to them, so they began to attend regularly. They were concerned about social issues and liked our church's social witness. They enjoyed the church's sense of community and participated in study and worship. Even though they both attended our membership exploration class several times, Jane had many doubts about the Christian faith. Learning about Christianity was much easier than making a commitment to Christ. Finally, her husband could wait no longer and decided to join the church without her.

A year later, Jane had a breakthrough in her thinking. Her searching mind had led her to resolve her questions, and she was ready to accept Jesus Christ as Lord and Savior and be baptized. With our pastor's assistance she wrote a baptismal liturgy that combined the historic words of the church with her own expression of what this act meant to her.

She invited all the coworkers in her office to worship with us that Sunday and to witness her baptism. When Jane came forward to confess her faith in Christ, she testified to the new life she was beginning. She knelt for baptism to symbolize the dying and then stood with a radiant smile that expressed her rising to a new way of looking at life.

Jane was baptized! There was hardly a dry eye in the congregation because we all knew her struggle to reach that moment. After years of questioning and indecision, Jane had claimed a new identity. She knew who she was with a clear vision and purpose that she had never known before. She wanted everyone to know that she had become a new person. In accepting the claims of the Christian covenant, she would henceforth strive to "walk in newness of life."

Jane's experience illustrates the transforming power of Christ in our lives as embodied in baptism. In her we witnessed the change from old life in sin for self to new life in Christ for God and others that Paul describes in Romans 6.

LESSON PLAN

■ Ask group members how many remember their own baptism. Tell them that Martin Luther, when tempted to stray from the faith, used to pat his head where the holy water had been placed and remind himself, "I've been baptized."

Encourage members to share their memories of baptisms—either their own baptism or that of others in their family or congregation. Begin with your own baptismal memories, with the story of Jane above, or with my experience in the baptistry at Emwas. As each experience is shared, ask: *What does baptism signify? Why is it important? How is God active in it?* Use these questions to lead into a discussion of Romans 6:3-4.

Then, drawing on the commentary above and the material in the student book [pages 31–37], lead the group in discussion using the questions below.

(1) *How do you define sin?* There are two common understandings of sin: (1) specific acts like drinking alcohol or engaging in racial discrimination or sexual misconduct and (2) anything that separates us from God. Another definition is "our failure to be what God created us to be." The Greek word for sin is *harmartia*, which means "missing the mark." Aspects of sin described in the Bible include failure to be what we are intended to be, the condition of guilt, deliberate breaking of the law, rebellion against God, violation of the covenant, ritualistic or moral uncleanliness, broken relationships, conscious evil or wickedness, the misuse of freedom, willful self-assertion, the negation of love, and alienation from God.

Ask the group for their definitions of *sin*, writing the definitions on a chalkboard or on a large sheet of paper as the members give them. Then compare those understandings with the ones given above, leading the group in developing a definition on which all can agree.

(2) *"How does your Christian faith help you to resist sin?"* [student book; page 34].

In the section in the lesson in the student book entitled "Walk in Newness of Life," the phrases "new life," "life in the Spirit," "a new being," and "a new creation" are used to refer to the life in Christ freed from the dominion of sin. Ask the group what holds them steady in this life of holiness and righteousness. Have them share experiences in which the helps they mentioned were present. List the resources they mention on a chalkboard or on a large sheet of paper. Among those that could be cited are: (1) trust in the power of God to sustain us; (2) the support of fellow Christians; (3) prayer and meditation; (4) regular Bible reading and memorization; (5) the example of stalwart Christians, both those in church history—Teresa of Avila, Martin Luther, Fannie Lou Hamer, Albert Schweitzer, and Oscar Romero, for example—and persons of our acquaintance; (6) sharing and prayer groups; (7) services of worship and the sacraments; (8) having a spiritual guide or counselor; (9) reading religious books; (10) acknowledging our weakness and confessing our sin.

(3) *"How does the knowledge that God is love help us cope with sin?"* [student book; page 35].

In the student book section entitled "United in Life and Death," we read that "in life or death we are forever surrounded by the matchless love of God." We tend to respond to those who love us by doing what they want us to do. Children strive to obey and please their parents, to win their approval, to be in a right relationship with them. Likewise, we show our gratitude for God's love by resisting the temptation to disappoint and dishonor God. We know that God will forgive us when we fail if we seek his pardon. But we would rather not sin in the first place; we would rather rest in God's love and power to overcome our selfish tendencies. Knowing that there is One on whom we can always depend gives us the strength to look evil in the eye and say, "No!"

(4) *"How has God's grace helped sanctify your life?"* [student book; page 36].

This question refers to the issue of sanctification discussed in Romans 6:20-23. Review the treatment of sanctification in the "Sanctified Slaves" section of the lesson in the student book so the group members understand that holiness is both divine gift and human responsibility. Sanctification is not so changeable as feelings, which come and go with moods of joy and depression. Rather, sanctification is a condition bestowed on us by God when we accept Christ, a condition that we must cultivate and develop.

If we have been utilizing the resources of faith listed in Question 2 and have been resting in God's love as mentioned in Question 3, we will be continuing to "grow in grace" and "move on to perfection" (Wesley). We may not always feel holy, but we know that the God who has sanctified us will nurture the seed of faith in our souls. Evidences of this will be our practice of both the spiritual disciplines (prayer, worship, Bible study, and so forth) and deeds of moral integrity and caring service, as mentioned in the discussion of Romans 6:20-23.

(5) *What can you do to help someone you know return to the holy life?* Paul's advice for dealing with sinners ranges between two extremes: rejection and expulsion from the community (1 Corinthians 5:11-13) and patience, hospitality, support, and encouragement (Romans 15:1-2, 7). Ask the group for examples of when they or others slipped or failed and how the church responded.

Share the following story with your group:

Teresa had two school age children when she finally decided to divorce her abusive husband. She felt hurt, guilty, and depressed. One night in a fit of despondency she went into the bathroom and slashed her wrists. Her attempted suicide brought the whole problem out into the open; and she was sure that, disgraced as she was, she would never be welcomed back into the church. But, wonder of wonders, church people visited her in the hospital, prayed with and for her, cared for her children, and urged her to look to the church as a resource in her time of need. In these and other ways, they let her know that they would stand with her through it all because she was a child of God and a Christian friend.

This response was a conversion experience for Teresa. She moved from being someone who had gone to church because she was raised that way and for the good of her children to someone who met God's grace in the loving acts of Christian friends and dedicated her life to serving Christ. Her first step, after she recovered, was to work with the youth in her church. She had learned literally the meaning of "the wages of sin is death, but the free gift of God [as mediated to her by the church] is eternal life in Christ Jesus our Lord."

Close the session by calling attention to how Christ's death and resurrection made possible victory over sin and death for people like Jane, Teresa, and all of us. Lead the group in singing "Beneath the Cross of Jesus." Then ask group members to offer sentence prayers of gratitude for God's gifts of salvation (justification) and holiness (sanctification) through Christ.

[1] From *Romans*, by Robert Jewett, Volume 22 in the Cokesbury Basic Bible Commentary (Graded Press, 1988); pages 72–73.

TRY ANOTHER METHOD

■ Before the session begins, prepare a list of the theological terms that have been used thus far in the study, which may seem strange or unfamiliar to some group members—*salvation, grace, faith, reconciliation, righteousness, sin, justification, sanctification, holiness, eternal life, baptism,* and any others you think may be troublesome.

Distribute pencils and paper and give the members a "word association test," asking them to write the first thought that comes into their mind as you read aloud each of the words. Then discuss together the members' responses to each word, introducing ideas from your reading of the material above and explanations in word books and Bible dictionaries.

Stress that although these words have technical theological meanings, they have been part of the vocabulary of faith down through Christian history. People of faith today need to have a working knowledge of them even though they may not often use them in everyday conversation.

Because some group members will not have had a church background, take care to affirm everyone's responses as reflecting an aspect of truth. Fresh insights sometimes come from persons who are hearing these words in their biblical context for the first time.

Chapter Five

SHARING CHRIST'S GLORY

PURPOSE

To remind us that as children of God we share in the hope of resurrection

BIBLE PASSAGE

Romans 8:9-17

> ### CORE VERSES
> We are . . . heirs of God and joint heirs with Christ—if, in fact, we suffer with him so that we may also be glorified with him. (Romans 8:16-17)

GET READY

■ In addition to the lesson material and Scripture passage for this week, read a commentary on the passage and an article on "Assurance" in a Bible dictionary or word book.

Reflect on the questions in the lesson in the student book and prepare your answers.

Finally, alert members with adoption experience to be ready to share in relation to Question 4.

BIBLE BACKGROUND

■ In Romans 8, we come to the climax of Paul's argument in his letter. It is one of the greatest chapters in the entire Bible, emphasizing the power of the Holy Spirit in helping believers overcome evil both within and without. Basic themes are the contrast between flesh and spirit (verses 1-11), our adoption as children of God through the work of the Spirit (verses 12-17, 26-27), hope for the redemption of the whole creation (verses 18-25), the providence of God (verses 28-30), and God's power in overcoming all obstacles (verses 31-39). The chapter contains no moral commands; in the life of the Spirit only the guidance of God is needed. The chapter opens with "no condemnation" (verse 1); ends with no separation (verse 39); and in between proclaims the Spirit's conquest of sin, death, flesh, decay, and other perils (verses 35-39). These ideas relate closely to the themes of conversion, holiness, the Spirit's assurance of salvation, and the battle to defeat personal and social sin. The chapter is outlined as follows:

(A) Liberation From Sin and Death (verses 1-4)
(B) Struggle Between Flesh and Spirit (5-11)
(C) Adoption Into God's Family (12-17)
(D) Salvation of All Creation (18-25)
(E) The Spirit's Assistance in Weakness (26-27)
(F) God's Good Purpose and Plan (28-30)
(G) Constancy in God's Love (31-39)

We deal with verses 9-17 now and with verses 1-11 in the next lesson.

Romans 8:9-12. The verses in our Bible Lesson stress the Spirit's role in convincing us that we are accepted into God's family. In Romans 8:11, Paul links the suffering and glory of the Christian life with Christ's death and resurrection. In verses 9-10, Paul describes the benefits of Christ's gift of new life in terms of the Spirit's power to aid us in overcoming flesh, fear, and slavery to sin. The term *flesh,* used here interchangeably with the word *body,* does not mean simply our physical nature but rather the self-centered "self," which is motivated by desire, pride, and willful pursuit of one's own well-being. In Chapter 7, Paul views the self as made up of three elements—reason, which is the location of God's law; flesh, the source of base desire; and will, which chooses between God's purpose and lawless desire. This is similar to Freud's understanding of the self as composed of the ego, superego, and id; with the id, like Paul's "flesh," being the urges to which we are in bondage. In Romans 8:12, Paul is saying that Christian brothers and sisters are not compelled to live by the desires of the flesh; such a life is not an option for the faithful.

Verse 13. Rather, we are called to rely on the power of the Spirit to put behind us desire and the acts that issue from it. This makes the difference between life and death. This contrast between works of the flesh and the fruit of the Spirit is made plain in Galatians 5:16-26. There Paul uses the phrase "desires of the flesh" to include sins and impure acts, which are both physical (fornication, drunkenness) and spiritual (idolatry, jealousy). The "fruits of the spirit" include self-control (of those desires). To have life, we must seek the Spirit's aid in mortifying (putting to death) the "*mis*deeds" of the flesh.

Verses 14-15. If we allow the Spirit to guide us, we become identified as children of God, adopted into the divine family. This brings us into such a close relationship with God that we can address the Almighty as "Abba," which is the Aramaic equivalent of "Daddy" or "Papa." This deep sense of belonging as full members of God's family is different from the "spirit of slavery" and the "fear" that slaves would feel in the presence of their masters. While the distance between God and humans is much greater than that between master and slave, that gap is bridged by Christ's forgiveness and the Spirit's power overcoming the pull of selfish desires. Because our sin has removed us from the intimacy of God's family, we no longer feel we belong. Therefore we must be adopted back in through the Spirit's enabling work.

The verb *cry* perhaps reflects the ecstasy of early Christian worship, in which speaking in tongues (1 Corinthians 14) was sometimes employed by the poor, oppressed, marginalized people who often made up the house churches. For these persons speaking in tongues was an expression of the joy of being fully accepted by the heavenly Creator. Those separated from loved ones and rejected by society through the abuses of Roman slavery, poverty, and exploitation had good reason for ecstatic rejoicing when loved by One greater than Caesar, One who invited them to call him "Daddy."

And we, likewise accepted and loved as true children of God, can also call God *Abba.*

Verses 16-17. These verses proclaim that the Spirit assures us in our hearts that we are children and heirs of God, having a place in the heavenly family alongside Christ. The inclusive phrase "children of God" indicates that the sense of belonging to the family of God includes women as well as men, an aspect of the early Christian community that put it at odds with the practice of both Jew and Gentile throughout the Roman Empire. This is similar to the radical equality of women and men, clergy and laity, rich and poor, proclaimed and practiced in the Base Christian Communities of Latin America—in contrast to the norms of their classist, sexist, and sometimes racist society. All persons, regardless of birth, status, or income, says Paul, are respected members of the household of God and are to be treated with honor and dignity (See also Galatians 3:28.).

The closing phrase of verse 17 provides a transition to the rest of the chapter. If we are willing to take up our cross and follow Christ as he commanded us (Matthew 16:24), we will have to face the hardships of life, hardships that result precisely from our commitment to follow Christ. No one desires to suffer, but we are ready to face these difficulties because of the transforming work of the Spirit in our hearts.

OUR NEED

■ Indiana Acevedo was the *coordinadora* of her Base Christian Community in the Barrio San Judas, Managua, Nicaragua. In addition to being a single mother with six children, Indiana served each morning as a volunteer social worker with a school for street children, making house visits by bus or on foot all over the city. In the afternoons and evenings, she worked in her Base Community, supervising programs in health care, nutrition, cholera prevention, preparation of soy meals for children and mothers, preschool education, youth activities, sex education, sewing instruction, Bible study, and church membership training. She also worked with twenty families in a shantytown in another part of the city where displaced people lived in hastily constructed shacks.

When I asked Indiana what motivated her investment in these varied forms of service, she said, "My commitment of faith. I learned in the Bible that faith without action is dead. God calls me to serve, and I do so with happiness and dedication. I find the presence of God among the people. In the midst of difficulties God is there. Jesus is the center of our life, and we meet Jesus in the Bible."

One night each week Indiana met with other members of her Base Community in one of their homes to pray, sing, study the Bible, discuss the Scripture's relationship to daily life, and plan and coordinate service activities. She was educated, but most members were not. All were poor; the majority were women. A priest attended occasionally, but the leadership was firmly in the hands of the laity. They attended the parish church on Sunday. Each Monday evening Indiana participated in a training, coordinating, and planning meeting with leaders from twenty-two other Base Communities in Managua. Together they studied, prayed, and discussed how they could apply their Christian faith to the growing problems of poverty, unemployment, illness, conflict, malnutrition, and despair in postwar Nicaragua.

When I visited several of these communities, I was profoundly impressed with their similarity to the early house churches in Rome, that is, with their deep faith, hope, and commitment under severe conditions of poverty, oppression, and marginalization. They lived a resurrection hope surrounded by death and discouragement. They had looked into the tomb; found it empty; seen the angel; and heard the message to "go, tell." They had put aside selfish desire in order to serve the needs of others. They were clearly aware of their dignity as full members of the family of God and were not afraid to call God *Abba*. They will be glorified with Christ because they have suffered with him. Truly, the Spirit witnesses with their spirits, as with mine, that they, like the Roman Christians, are children of God. I know better what it means to be the church for having met these "heirs of God and joint heirs with Christ."

LESSON PLAN

■ Ask group members to recall past Easter experiences along the lines of the story that begins the lesson in the student book. Sporting new outfits as a child, sanctuaries lined with lilies, special Easter music, hope and encouragement received in funeral services, packed churches, and sunrise services may be mentioned. Then lead the group in discussion using the questions below.

(1) *"What does the celebration of the Resurrection mean to you, personally?"* [student book; page 41].

Ask each person for his or her answer to this question. Start off with your own. Write the gist of each person's comment on a chalkboard or on a large sheet of paper. Supplement group responses with the following:

To believe in the Resurrection means that Jesus is not just a historical figure; he is present with us as the Lord of new life. To believe in the Resurrection means that we do not just learn about Jesus; we can come to know Jesus as our personal Savior and Lord. To believe in the Resurrection means that sin and death are not the last word; Jesus has conquered them both and given us the gift of eternal life. To believe in the Resurrection means that hardship and disappointment, difficulty and loss, need not defeat us; the risen Christ gives us strength and hope to overcome them. To believe in the Resurrection means that we cannot keep silent about our faith in a living Lord.

(2) *"How do you feel about the use of Easter (or Christmas) as a celebration of material excess and/or an exhibition of finery?"* [student book; page 42].

With regard to Easter finery, you might find two points of view on this question. Some people may feel that the wearing of bright, new suits and dresses on Easter, as well as the decoration of sanctuaries with lilies and special banners, is a fitting expression of the Easter joy. In springtime the crocuses peek forth, the grass turns green, baby chicks and bunnies remind us of the miracle of new life. God is decking out the world in Easter splendor; why shouldn't we humans get into the spirit as well?

Others will argue that the real meaning of Easter is spiritual, not material. Many people spend exorbitant sums for new clothes just to join the Easter parade and show themselves off. Such self-centered vanity caters to the desires of the flesh or "deeds of the body," which Christians are supposed to "put to death" (Romans 8:13). Followers of Jesus are called to "deny themselves and take up their cross and follow me" (Mark 8:34). If we expect to "be glorified with him" (Romans 8:17), we must suffer with him.

If only one of these positions is raised, bring up the other yourself and make sure that both are given serious consideration.

(3) *"What do you value most about your adopted family in Christ?"* [student book; page 43].

If any group members are adopted or have adopted children, ask them to share what this experience has been like for them. Although some adopted children may not feel as fully accepted as those with a blood relationship to their parents, others, whose parents have stressed that "we chose you" or "we picked you out," feel fully loved and affirmed. Clearly, Paul has the latter in mind when he uses the analogy of "a spirit of adoption" (Romans 8:15) for the inclusion of believers in the family of God.

The adopted family in Christ refers to the church, the community of faith, the fellowship of believers. Ask members to name the qualities they appreciate about this or other congregations. List these qualities on a chalkboard or on a large sheet of paper as the group members mention them. Aspects one might suggest include: inspiring worship, caring people, dedicated service, friendly welcome, fair treatment, trusting climate, spiritual nurture, safe environment for children and youth, witness of integrity, firm stand for justice, continual work for peace, inclusive community. Refer to Indiana Acevedo and the Base Christian Communities as an example of the power of such an "adopted family" to transform lives and serve society.

(4) *"How and when have you felt the Spirit's assurance that you are a child of God?"* [student book; page 44].

The student book section entitled "The Spirit's Witness" answers the question, "How do we know we are saved?" with Paul's emphasis in Romans 8:16 on the witness of the Spirit. The student book describes this witness as "that inner voice that affirms we are accepted." John Wesley, founder of Methodism, troubled for years by doubts as to whether he really was a child of God, felt his "heart strangely warmed" in his conversion at Aldersgate and never doubted it again. The hymns "Blessed Assurance, Jesus Is Mine" and "How Can We Sinners Know" express the believer's confidence in the "Spirit bearing witness with our spirit that we are children of God." We can feel that presence within.

Ask persons to share times when they have felt this sense of assurance that God was with them and loved them. Experiences of conversion, worship, prayer, inspiration, calling, comfort, encouragement, hope, and guidance might be mentioned.

(5) *"What strengthens you in times of suffering with Christ?"* [student book; page 45].

This question grows out of the student book section

"If We Suffer With Him," based on the Key Verse, which speaks of the kinds of suffering, physical and psychological, that test our faith. Suffering also includes being the victim of ridicule and opposition, which is clearly part of what Paul had in mind.

Invite the group to describe experiences of suffering and the faith resources that have sustained them during such times. List these experiences on a chalkboard or on a large sheet of paper as the group members mention them. Scripture, prayer, the comfort and support of friends, the sense of God's abiding presence, the discipline of self-denial, the hope of relief, the prayers of others, a favorite hymn, and receiving the sacraments are sources of strength that group members may mention.

To close the session, have the group sing "Blessed Assurance." Then pray in unison the prayer printed at the end of the lesson in the student book.

TRY ANOTHER METHOD

■ For Question 2 about Easter finery, form two small groups and have them develop arguments pro and con, respectively, using the ideas presented above. Then conduct a brief debate on the statement, "The wearing of fancy new clothes on Easter should be banned in our church."

For the questions calling for sharing of personal faith experience—(1) on the meaning of Easter, (3) on the value found in the church, (4) on the Spirit's assurance, and (5) on strength in suffering—form small groups of three persons. Let each group choose one of these questions to discuss. Have them take turns sharing an experience in answer to the question, with one of the other two taking the role of a "prophet"—confronting the teller with questions like, "Have you considered this?" "Why did you do that?" or "How could you have overlooked such and such?" The other person will take the role of "priest"—offering support, acceptance, and understanding to the teller with comments like, "You must have really been hurting/ grateful/angry/happy"; "I hear what you're saying"; or "God was really with you in that." When one has shared, shift roles so each gets the chance to be teller, prophet, and priest.

Allow about ten minutes total for this small group activity. Then call the entire group together to ask what members learned about resurrection joy, Christian community, the assurance of the Spirit, and the resources of faith. The assumption behind this approach is that spiritual learning can come through experience as well as through ideas.

Form the group into a Base Christian Community to discuss the biblical material, using the Base Community's three-step process for Bible study:

(1) *See.* What are the needs in our lives and world that cry out for the message of resurrection hope, the rejection of the desires of the flesh, and the witness of the Spirit?

(2) *Judge.* How does the verse-by-verse meaning of these passages speak to these needs?

(3) *Act.* What will we do to apply this message to those problems?

Chapter Six

LIVING IN THE SPIRIT

PURPOSE

To contrast living in the flesh and living in the Spirit

BIBLE PASSAGE

Romans 8:1-11

> ### CORE VERSE
> For the law of the Spirit of life in Christ Jesus has set you free from the law of sin and of death.
> (Romans 8:2)

GET READY

■ In addition to the Bible Lesson, read the articles on "Flesh," "Spirit," and "Flesh and Spirit" in a Bible dictionary or word book. Write on slips of paper some of the biblical references to flesh and spirit mentioned below.

Pray for the group members during the week, asking God to strengthen them in dealing with whatever compulsions to sin they are facing and to help them grow in the marks of the spiritual life.

The theme of this lesson is personal, so think through and decide the level at which it is appropriate to discuss with your group such topics as desires and urges, compulsions and addictions, spiritual qualities and virtues, and taking one's "spiritual temperature."

BIBLE BACKGROUND

■ This passage and lesson focus on the contrast between life in the flesh and life in the spirit. In conjunction with our Bible Lesson, you may wish to read Romans 7:14-25 and Acts 9:1-2; 22:3-5; 26:4-11 (references to Paul's pre-conversion experience) and commentaries on these passages. Finally, read Galatians 6:17.

The term *flesh* is used several different ways in the Bible to indicate the following: the soft bodily material (Job 10:11; Isaiah 31:3); the male sexual member (Genesis 17:9-14; Exodus 28:42); sexual union (Genesis 2:24) and procreation (John 1:13); living things (Genesis 6:13; 7:15-16; 1 Corinthians 15:39); kinship (Genesis 37:27; 2 Samuel 19:12-13); animal meat used in sacrifice (Leviticus 6:24-27); the frailty and imperfection of human nature (2 Corinthians 4:11); earthly descent (Romans 9:8); the human as contrasted with the divine (John 8:15; 1 Corinthians 1:26; 2 Corinthians 5:16; note that phrases such as *by human standards* read *according to the flesh* in the Greek text); the whole body or person (John 1:14); humanity or what is human (Isaiah 40:5; note that *all people* reads *all flesh* in Hebrew; Philippians 3:3-4); sensitivity (Ezekiel 11:19); superficiality (John 8:15); weakness (2 Chronicles 32:8; Psalm 56:4; Romans 8:3); and mortality (Psalm 78:39). Paul uses it to mean the urge or instrument of sin (Romans 7:24; Galatians 5:16-21).

John does not see the flesh or matter as evil but rather affirms its worthiness to receive the incarnation of God, the Word made flesh (John 1:14). He does, however, contrast flesh and spirit in terms of the new birth: "What is born of the flesh is flesh, and what is born of the Spirit is spirit" (John 3:6). First John also distinguishes between the spirits of truth and error that do and do not, respectively, confess that Jesus Christ has come in the flesh (1 John 4:1-6). The former are from God, the latter from the "spirit of the antichrist" (verse 3).

The Hebrew (*ruach*) and Greek (*pneuma*) words for "spirit" also may be translated "breath" or "wind." Spirit is what gives life to the physical body (Genesis 6:3; Numbers 16:22; 27:16; Ezekiel 37:1-14). The spirit is power in contrast to weakness (Zechariah 4:6; Acts 1:8); almighty God alongside weak humanity (Isaiah 31:3). Acceptable worship of God in the Spirit is preferred over fleshly attempts to please God (Philippians 3:3). Spirit struggles with flesh (fatigue) in the desire to pray (Mark 14:38).

Paul was absent in the flesh but present in spirit (Colossians 2:5). Both flesh and spirit can be contaminated by sin (2 Corinthians 7:1). In the Last Judgment the spirit will be saved but the flesh destroyed (1 Corinthians 5:5). Paul correlates the spirit with faith and the flesh with law (Galatians 3:2-3). He also contrasts Isaac, born free in the Spirit according to God's promise, with Ishmael, a slave born in the flesh, signifying the curse of the law (Galatians 4:21-31). The spiritual person is led by God's Spirit, while the fleshly person is an unbeliever (1 Corinthians 2:12–3:4). Vices are identified as works of the flesh, virtues with the fruit of the Spirit (Galatians 5:16-25)—the former bring death, the latter eternal life (Galatians 6:7-8; Romans 8:1-17).

A study of Romans 7:7-25 is essential to understanding Romans 8. Paul is describing his preconversion struggle with observance of the law (See Acts 9:1-2; 22:3-5; 26:4-11.). The law made him aware of sin and moral disobedience. This should not be blamed on the law, which in itself is good, but on the inclination to sin of every human being descended from Adam. Before his conversion, Paul was in agony due to conflict between his belief that the moral law was right and must be obeyed and his inability to live up to it because of his inner weakness.

J.B. Phillips paraphrases Paul's spiritual strife this way:

My own behavior baffles me. For I find myself not doing what I really want to do but doing what I really loathe. . . . But it cannot be said that 'I' am doing them at all—it must be sin that has made its home in my nature. . . . I often find that I have the will to do good, but not the power . . . . When I come up against the Law I want to do good, but in practice I do evil. My conscious mind wholeheartedly endorses the Law, yet I observe an entirely different principle at work in my nature. This is in continual conflict with my conscious attitude, and makes me an unwilling prisoner to the law of sin and death. In my mind I am God's willing servant, but in my own nature I am bound fast, as I say, to the law of sin and death. It is an agonizing situation, and who on earth can set me free from the clutches of my own sinful nature?[1]

How many of us can voice a similar complaint?

Romans 8:1-4. Neither the law nor any human effort or device can solve the problem. In Romans 7:25, Paul points to the only solution: "God through Jesus Christ our Lord." The grace of God in Christ both reveals human self-righteousness and offers forgiveness. It is no longer necessary to try to win God's favor by obeying the law. We must acknowledge that we fall far short of God's glory yet are loved unconditionally. God's acceptance provides a solid basis for genuine self-esteem and motivates us, not to boastful works of righteousness, but to holy living in grateful response to God's grace.

This point, discussed in Romans 3:21–4:25 and 6:1-23, is made explicit here. Christ frees us from the principle (law) of sin and death that plagues us on the inside. By sending the Son in human form (the flesh) and thus demonstrating that human life could be lived in the Spirit, God in Christ overcame the power of human desires (condemned sin in the flesh). Christ was human like us, yet he did not share in the human hostility to God and holy living. Rather, he unmasked our self-righteousness and separation from God, freed us from slavery to sin, and extended us pardon and a transformed life. Thus we can begin living, not by selfish desire, but by the Holy Spirit ("walk not according to the flesh but according to the Spirit").

Verses 5-9. The domains of flesh and Spirit are in continual conflict. "Flesh" here refers to a way of thinking and being that includes the choice of values and the action to realize those values. In relation to God, the flesh involves enmity and acts of defiance against God; it is complete self-centeredness. On this definition, "flesh" can also refer to those efforts to achieve by works what only God can achieve through grace. The self-centered need to prove themselves acceptable by good works. This brings death because it puts our righteousness into competition with the perfect goodness of Christ. But our attempt at self-justification is shattered by Christ, and the way is opened for holy living through the power of the Holy Spirit.

The "Spirit" is the Spirit of Christ, given to humans (verses 10 and 15-16) and expressed in both moral and charismatic ways. It is the sign of the new era of Christ, different from the old era of Adam. To live by the standards of the old era (the mind set on the flesh) is to reject God, as Paul knows he did prior to his conversion. Through his pride in obeying the law and persecuting Christians for rejecting circumcision and relying on grace, he had actually been rebelling against God. The "mind of the flesh" fosters arrogance, hostility, and dissension. It is set against the "mind of the Spirit," which admits to sinful tendencies but has qualities of "life" (hope, gratitude) and "peace" (harmony, trust) (verse 6). This Spirit enables us to see other people as brothers and sisters and thus can resolve the tensions in communities of faith, whether the Roman house churches or our contemporary congregations and institutions.

Verses 10-11. Because we have accepted Christ, our bodies, which had been deadened by sin, are renewed to new life in righteousness. The same God who raised Jesus gives us life in the Spirit. We have died to the old, as symbolized in our baptism (Romans 6:5). The power of sin has been destroyed by the Spirit of Christ who now fills us. It is not that the physical body is bad in itself but rather that our self-centered desires and passions use the body for evil ends (Romans 6:12-13). Our "mortal bodies" (Romans 8:11), however, can become Spirit-controlled and thus experience the joys of abundant life, which begins now but is everlasting.

OUR NEED

■ Beyers Naude was an Afrikaner; the son of a Boer War hero; and a founding member of the Broederbond, the secret society that invented and controlled South Africa's system of apartheid or white supremacy. As a prominent pastor in the Dutch Reformed Church, he reached the highest levels of South African society and was often mentioned as a future prime minister.

But, like Paul on the Damascus Road, Beyers Naude met the righteous and loving God in a Christian conversion experience; and his life was radically changed. From a darling of the Afrikaner elite, he was transformed into a committed opponent of apartheid and risked ostracism and persecution by his former friends. In 1963, he left the Dutch Reformed Church, which he deeply loved, preaching a farewell sermon on "Obedience to God"—as opposed to human law and custom. He had passed from death to life, from a mind set on things of the flesh to living by the Spirit, from acceptance of the principle of sin—the desire to preserve self and privilege—to life in the Spirit—a life of love, compassion, and respect for all God's children.

Beyers Naude then founded the Christian Institute, an interracial, interdenominational organization—declared illegal in 1977—that fostered Christian unity, racial justice, and opposition to apartheid. He was banned (placed under house arrest and excluded from all social activity) for seven years by the government and then became general secretary of the South African Council of Churches, where he spoke and acted for the gospel of love and justice. While attending a mass funeral for black victims of racial violence, he was lifted up on people's shoulders—a most unusual honor for a white person in South Africa.

When Beyers Naude spoke at our commencement years ago, I was deeply impressed by his integrity, humility, and courage. He said to us, "Ensure that your understanding of faith, of the gospel, of the message of Christ's liberation is clear, relevant, and comprehensive of the whole of humankind. . . . Make your Christian faith real, meaningful, vibrant, and relevant. . . . [Go] out to Christians and others, saying, 'We are one with you . . . in the realization of the tremendous potential for change that God has given . . . us. Let us build together so that we may truly make this world God's Kingdom.' "[2]

Naude could say with Paul, "I thank God there is a way out through Jesus Christ our Lord. No condemnation now hangs over the head of those who are 'in' Christ Jesus. For the new spiritual principal of life 'in' Christ Jesus lifts me out of the old vicious circle of sin and death."[3]

LESSON PLAN

■ Begin by asking the group the difference between flesh and spirit. Give out one or more slips of paper with Bible references to flesh and spirit to each group member; then have people look up the passages and read them aloud. Explain the different meanings given these words by different Scripture writers as noted above, finishing with Paul's interpretation in our passage.

Introduce Beyers Naude as an example of one who chose, after conversion to Christ, to live by the Spirit rather than by the flesh—at considerable personal risk.

Then, drawing on the commentary above and the material in the student book [pages 46–54], lead the group in discussion using the following questions.

(1) *Have you been tempted to judge your own spiritual strength by adding up acts of devotion or mercy?*

If so, what were the circumstances?

For us as well as for Paul, living by the law means counting our merits to prove our spirituality and holiness. We go to church, pay our taxes, serve our community, say our prayers, obey the law, stay out of trouble, tithe our income, treat others fairly, and say the Pledge of Allegiance and Lord's Prayer. We are not prejudiced, greedy, vicious, or nasty. We keep our grass cut, pay our bills, and do a good turn now and then. The list of our virtues is endless. With the Pharisee in the parable (Luke 18:9-14), we can say, "God, I thank you that I am not like other people." Surely, God must be pleased with us. This is being bound by the law of sin and death, from which only Christ can set us free (Romans 8:2).

Discuss when and how this attitude can affect us and/or the church.

(2) *"How do you combat the urge to seek satisfaction of personal desires at the expense of the fullness of spiritual life?"* [student book; page 49].

The student book comments on psychological compulsions [page 48]—to win, buy, have illicit sex, fight, be envious, and so forth—which is today's way of talking about setting our "minds on the things of the flesh" (Romans 8:5). Many people are speaking today about our "addictive society" in which both persons and institutions are caught up in behaviors that are unmanageable. Addicts are those who have no control over a particular substance or habit in their lives and whose involvement with it puts them on a downward slide leading to death. These addictions include drinking alcohol and using other drugs, gambling, eating, spending, committing acts of violence, working, and playing.

Those who work with addicted persons describe them as self-centered, dishonest, and obsessive. They tend to get in deeper and deeper until they become dominated by their desires, losing their sense of values and morality. They cut themselves off from input from family and friends. Their inner lives are confused and out of control, while they at the same time try to control those upon whom they depend. They are troubled and dysfunctional. People who support addicts in their self-destructive behavior are called co-dependents; and some of those who suffer the harmful effects of their mutually damaging relationship are now themselves seeking treatment, for example, as Adult Children of Alcoholics. Addictive patterns are passed from one generation to the next in the form of low self-esteem, the need to be needed, and lack of self-discipline. It is estimated that over ninety percent of Americans are affected by addiction in one or the other of these roles. This includes most of us. So we have no trouble saying with Paul, "Wretched [one] that I am! Who will rescue me from this body of death? . . . With my flesh I am a slave to the law of sin. . . . To set the mind on the flesh is death" (Romans 7:24-25; 8:6).

But we can also rejoice with Paul: "Thanks be to God through Jesus Christ our Lord! . . . There is therefore now no condemnation for those who are in Christ Jesus. For the law of the Spirit of life in Christ Jesus has set [me] free from the law of sin and of death" (Romans 7:25; 8:1-2). Among the twelve steps to overcoming addiction are two we can learn from Paul—admitting our inability to change and relying on a Higher Power.

Ask the group members to share their struggles with desires, addictions, and compulsions and how they have learned to deal with them. Ask any involved in Twelve Step programs to tell how they are being helped and what spiritual lessons are to be learned from this process.

(3) *"How would you define the difference between a religious fanatic and a person living in the Spirit?"* [student book; page 50].

No doubt many in the Dutch Reformed Church in South Africa saw Beyers Naude as a fanatic. But we may consider Beyers Naude a saint. By what standard shall we judge? Paul gives us the guideline in Romans 8:9: "Anyone who does not have the Spirit of Christ does not belong to him." The Spirit of Christ is one of love. Beyers Naude acted out of love for his black brothers and sisters. The sanity and integrity of persons who devote themselves to prayer, doing good, serving others, or changing unjust systems can be judged by how fully they are living in the spirit of love.

(4) *What do you think are some marks of the spiritual life?* Address this question to the group, recording their answers on a chalkboard or on a large sheet of paper. Ask for examples of each mark of the spiritual life. Supplement their discussion with ideas from the student book. The student book mentions four attributes of spirituality: love for God, human charity, purity, and humility. In the section following in the student book, relying on Paul, the writer adds peace, tolerance, righteousness, and seeking the good. The life of Beyers Naude exhibits the traits of integrity, courage, and resistance to evil. Look up Paul's lists of Christian virtues in Galatians 5:22-23, Philippians 4:8-9, and Colossians 3:12-17 for still other qualities. Discuss how Christians can cultivate these characteristics.

(5) *"Take stock: How well do you measure up to the standard of life in the Spirit?"* [student book; page 53].

I once participated in a group in which, during our closing worship each day, each person was asked, "Have you been faithful today?" We were to answer either, "Yes and no" or "No and yes." Some of us are more faithful than others. We are more faithful some days than others. No one embodies these qualities perfectly. Each of us needs the grace and strength of God to "walk not according to the flesh but according to the Spirit" (Romans 8:4).

If the group is willing, go around the circle and ask each member to respond either "Yes and no" or "No and yes" to the question, Did you walk in the Spirit last week?

To close the session, call for "popcorn prayers," beginning with the petition, "Spirit of God, give us . . ." and asking members to call out a word or phrase describing the mark of the spiritual life that they most need right now. Close with the chorus "Spirit of the Living God."

[1]From *The New Testament in Modern English,* revised edition, by J.B. Phillips. © J.B. Phillips 1958, 1960, 1972. Used by permission of Macmillan Publishing Co., Inc.
[2]From *Cloud of Witnesses,* edited by Jim Wallis and Joyce Hollyday (Orbis Books, Sojourners, 1991); pages 163–64.
[3]From *The New Testament in Modern English,* revised edition, by J.B. Phillips.

TRY ANOTHER METHOD

■ In the paragraphs above, Question 1 describes a legalist, Question 2 an addict, Question 3 a fanatic, and Question 4 a saint. Ask four group members to take these four roles and to discuss in a fish bowl (in four chairs in the center of the room with the rest of the group surrounding them) several moral and spiritual dilemmas that contemporary Christians are facing. That is, the four persons will bring the perspectives of these four approaches to life to bear on some contemporary problems. For instance, if the issue were whether to give prizes for Sunday school attendance and Bible memorization, the legalist might argue that we should give such rewards because it would boost attendance and make our church look good. The addict might say that anything that develops a habit should be encouraged. The religious fanatic might contend that getting people to memorize the Bible, by whatever means, will make them better Christians. The saint would insist that the motive for coming to church and studying the Bible should be love of God, not hope of material reward.

If group members are slow to suggest dilemmas, propose the following: accepting someone into church membership who is a social drinker, feeling led to speak to someone about Christ but holding back out of fear or embarrassment, feeling guilty for not having daily devotions, feeling embarrassed about having a son or daughter who is living with someone outside of marriage, younger and older members in disagreement over church policies, not wanting to welcome all persons into the church.

Debrief the discussion of each issue with this question to the participants: *How did you feel in this role?* and with these questions to the group: *How did the contrast in approaches help clarify the issue?*

What is the faithful resolution to this dilemma?

What is God saying to us in this discussion?

Change persons in the roles after each discussion so all members have opportunity to take an active part.

Chapter Seven

USING GIFTS TO SERVE

PURPOSE

To help us appreciate and make use of the diversity of gifts of ministry within the body of Christ

BIBLE PASSAGE

Romans 12:1-18
Background: Romans 12

CORE VERSE

We have gifts that differ according to the grace given to us. (Romans 12:6)

GET READY

■ Begin your preparation by reading Romans 12 in several different versions and translations. Arrange to have several versions in your class setting. Also read the other passages about gifts: 1 Corinthians 12:8-11; Ephesians 2:8-10; 4:11; 1 Peter 4:10-11 and at least one commentary on Romans 12.

Take the "test" with which the lesson opens in the student book. Have paper and pencils on hand and, if you plan to use the optional methods, the 3 x 5 cards for the "strength bombardment." Pray that the group members trust one another enough to talk openly about their own and one another's gifts.

BIBLE BACKGROUND

■ Romans 12 marks the transition from the doctrinal to the ethical and practical section of the letter. The two are closely related, in that the letter as a whole focuses on the righteousness of God and 12:1–15:13 discusses the implications of God's righteousness for human behavior. This material is not just a collection of ethical guidelines but rather a carefully constructed argument for Christian living in response to God's gift of grace and justification by faith in Christ.

Romans 12:1-2. The motivation for righteous living is the appeal to "the mercies of God," which sums up the central theme of Romans 1–11. The Christian life is not a legalistic attempt to earn merits but a grateful response to God's love. Israel's faithful response to God's action on their behalf was to offer animal sacrifices; ours is to present ourselves as a living sacrifice. Our "spiritual worship" ("reasonable service" in King James, "intelligent worship" in Phillips, "the worship offered by mind and heart" or "the worship which you, as rational creatures, should offer" in the *New English Bible*) is to consecrate our bodies (total selves) to God. We are to offer our whole lives in thanksgiving to God—our relationships and responsibilities, our work and play, our joys and sorrows, both physical and spiritual activities. Here body and soul, which are often separated, are united. Christian worship is to be focused not only in the house church or sanctuary but also in our everyday life in the world.

While serving God in the world, we are not to conform to its values and standards of behavior. Our moral lives are to be lived, not in passive acceptance of others' rules and expectations just to win their approval, but in grateful response to God's grace that transforms us and our mental outlook. This inner change affects both our motivation and our capacity to understand God's will. To rely on human regulations and rulers to tell us what is right is to go back to conformity to the law. But, thanks to our new freedom in Christ, we need only seek God's leading in prayer and worship to have our thinking renewed.

The "you" in verse 2 is plural, which suggests that discerning the good, acceptable, and perfect will of God is not an individual task but must be done together within the community of faith. The combined wisdom of the congregation is needed to correct any false or misleading tendencies of individuals.

Verses 3-8. Some Christians overvalue their gifts and contributions to the church; others do not respect enough their worth and value to the body. This must have been a problem in the Roman house churches as well as today, for Paul here addresses both tendencies by emphasizing his authority ("the grace given to me") as the apostle to the Gentiles.

He attacks the first tendency, pride, in verse 3 by cautioning believers not to "cherish exaggerated ideas of yourself or your importance, but try to have a sane estimate of your capabilities."[1] In his commentary Robert Jewett translates this as "not to be superminded above what one ought to be minded, but to set your mind on being soberminded, each according to the measuring rod of faith that God has dealt out."[2] That is, realizing we are saved by grace, we must avoid a sense of superiority and pride in our achievements, which would be conforming to this world. Instead, we must recognize our limitations and understand that all our gifts are to be measured in light of the greatest of God's gifts to us—the gift of faith in Jesus Christ.

The opposite tendency, to undervalue ourselves out of a false sense of humility, is taken up in verses 4-8 through Paul's emphasis on the value of all members' gifts within the body of Christ. Paul does not rank these contributions in numerical order (as he does in 1 Corinthians 12:28) nor does he even mention status positions assigned to individuals, like apostle, pastor, evangelist (as in Ephesians 4:11). Rather, he here refers to functions in the church—prophecy, ministry, teaching, exhorting, giving, leading, cheering up. He asks Christians to do these things to the best of the ability God has given them. Because we belong to Christ, we belong to one another in his body (verse 4) and are called to use these gifts (verse 6, Revised Standard Version) to "equip the saints for the work of ministry" and to strengthen and upbuild the whole body (Ephesians 4:12). The contributions of every member,

though different, are equally important to the well-being of the whole (Romans 12:5).

Verses 9-13. The qualities mentioned here are all relational. Paul is describing the nature of relationships expected in a church as the body of Christ where all are "members one of another" (verse 5). The foundation stone of a congregational ethic is genuine love (verse 9)—a love that struggles for good and against evil (verse 9); is tender and respectful (verse 10); enthusiastic and devoted in service (verse 11); hopeful, patient, determined in prayer (verse 12); generous and friendly (verse 13).

As Christians, we are to put the grace we have received from God into practice, first of all in our relationships with fellow believers. This involves taking firm stands on issues of right and wrong (verse 9) and mutual caring and esteem of one another regardless of differences of opinion (verse 10). Such practical grace is spiritually rooted in fervent worship and committed service (verse 11). It produces joy, spiritual discipline, and steady endurance under hardship (verse 12) as well as a willingness to give sacrificially to meet the needs of fellow believers and outsiders alike (verse 13). This latter quality was particularly needed in Rome at the time; those returning from the exile under the edict of Claudius needed to be reintegrated into the community.

Verses 14-21. Although our printed Scripture only goes to Romans 12:18, this paragraph should be taken as a whole, as all of it relates to issues the churches in Rome were facing in dealing with the returning refugees. These refugees had been driven away under persecution and displaced while gone; they naturally felt some resentment. Action based on these feelings would be conformity to the world (Romans 12:2) and would violate the new life in Christ and the gifts of the Spirit stressed earlier. To manifest transformed minds (verse 2) would mean: loving, not hating, those who mistreated them (verse 14); celebrating with and consoling one another (verse 15); living peacefully with one another (sometimes at very close quarters in the Roman tenements) and accepting one another without conceit and regardless of economic or educational status (verse 16); not returning tit for tat but nobly rising above such vindictiveness (verse 17); and not taking revenge on enemies but unselfishly serving their bodily needs (verses 19-20; see Proverbs 25:21-22).

Such encouragement of strong but forgiving love stands in stark contrast to the prevailing emphasis on revenge and rebellion advocated by many Jewish contemporaries of Paul in these years just before the A.D.

66–70 Jewish-Roman war. "Modeling their behavior on the heroic tales in the Old Testament, they believed that vengeance against evildoers would achieve divine ends. In particular [they] . . . felt that the Roman governing authorities should be opposed on principle, and with force."[3] So it is understandable that those in Rome to whom Paul was writing might be tempted to take it upon themselves to wreak God's vengeance on Israel's oppressors.

But Paul summarizes his ethical appeal by asserting that Christian love calls for us not to stoop to the wicked standards of others trying to harm us but rather to demonstrate that love is more powerful than hate (verse 21). Or, as Phillips puts it, "Don't allow yourself to be overpowered by evil. Take the offensive—overpower evil with good!"[4] Doing so may lead our persecutors to regret and repent their evil ("heap burning coals on their heads" [verse 20]); but as Paul has emphasized in Romans 5:3-5 and 8:18-25, we cannot count on any such sudden and easy reversal. Because the old era of sin and violence is still with us, we must trust in God for strength in the present and hope for Christ's ultimate triumph in the era to come.

OUR NEED

■ Paul's ethic of a transformed mind expressed in redemptive love and resistance to evil was found in four Roman Catholic women who were martyred in El Salvador in December, 1980. Sisters Ita Ford, Maura Clarke, Dorothy Kazel, and layworker Jean Donovan, who had gone to El Salvador to work with the poor and with war refugees, were stopped at a military roadblock, taken to a remote spot, brutally raped, shot, and buried in a shallow grave.

About her work with the poor in Latin America, Sister Ita said, "Am I willing to suffer with the people here, the powerless? Can I say to my neighbors, 'I have no solutions to this situation; I don't know the answers, but I will walk with you, search with you, be with you?' Can I let myself be evangelized by this opportunity?"[5] Sister Maura, who had previously worked with Base Christian Communities in poor barrios in Nicaragua, was described by friends as "outstanding in her generosity."[6] Sister Dorothy had served with Native Americans in Arizona before going to El Salvador to minister to refugees. Realizing that her work was getting risky, she told a friend, "If a day comes when others will have to understand (if something happens to one of us), please explain it for me."[7] Dissatisfied with her affluent lifestyle and promising career in the U.S., Jean decided to become a missionary and was stirred by the faith and hope of the Salvadoran people in the midst of violence and poverty.

In paying tribute to these martyrs of the faith, Jesuit priest Jon Sobrino wrote,

Maura, Ita, Dorothy, and Jean are the dead Christ today. But they are also the risen Christ, who keeps alive the hope of liberation. . . . As Christians we believe that salvation comes to us through Jesus, but . . . salvation [also] comes to us through all men and women who love the truth better than lies, who are readier to give than to receive, who regard it as the highest form of love to give one's life rather than to keep it for oneself. Here God is present. Therefore, although these four bodies fill us with grief and indignation, our last word must be: thank you. With Maura, Ita, Dorothy, and Jean, God has passed through El Salvador.[8]

These four women lived and died by Paul's ethic of practical grace set forth in Romans 12. They were committed Christians who refused to conform to the world of evil and injustice around them; they were transformed by the renewal of their minds; they offered their bodies as a living sacrifice. In grateful response to God's grace in their lives and in the lives of their Salvadoran sisters and brothers, they used their gifts to serve and build up the church of the poor. They were not overcome by evil but gave their lives to overcome evil with good.

LESSON PLAN

■ Begin by distributing the different Bible translations to group members. Ask several to read aloud Romans 12:1-2. Then compare the different renderings.

Explore the meaning of the phrases "mercies of God," "present your bodies," "living sacrifice," "spiritual worship," "conformed to this world," "transformed by the renewing of your minds," and "discern . . . the will of God" in light of the various wordings and the "Hearing the Word" section above.

Tell the story of Ita, Maura, Dorothy, and Jean as an example of persons embodying the message of these two verses and the entire chapter.

Next, distribute pencils and paper and ask the group to take the "test" in the student book [pages 56–57]. Then lead a discussion on their responses in light of the following questions:

What gifts has God given you personally? Ask each member to mention, from the "test" or from their general self-awareness, at least one gift that they feel God has given them. If some members are reluctant to do so, ask others in the group to identify their gifts for them. List these gifts on a chalkboard or on a large sheet of paper.

What gifts are present in our group? When the list is complete, comment on the impressive number and diversity of gifts present in the group as a whole.

How can our gifts be used to build up the body of Christ in our congregation and community? Before the group answers this question, list on a chalkboard or on a large sheet of paper the needs known to be present in the lives of individuals, families, community, and world. Then correlate the gifts in your group with these needs. Examples might include: Construction skills could help provide housing for the homeless; music abilities could enrich the choir; the gift of cooking could be offered to a soup kitchen; financial resources could assist a mission project; training in drama could help a group of physically or mentally disadvantaged persons put on a play; computer skills might help put the church "on line" for financial and membership records; "people skills" could provide support and care to folks in crisis.

How do our gifts compare with those in Paul's time? Have the group compare the lists of gifts in the "test" and on the chalkboard or large piece of paper with those in Romans 12:6-8; 1 Corinthians 12:8-11; Ephesians 4:11; 1 Peter 4:10-11. Ask: W*hich items were hardest to match?*

How have times changed or remained the same with regard to the need for these gifts?

In this discussion emphasize that (1) Christians and their gifts are all of equal value in God's sight; (2) spiritual gifts are not limited to the lists in these Scripture passages but include the abilities in the "test" and many others; (3) the church is weakened whenever even one person does not contribute the gift God has given him or her; (4) gifts are neither to be boasted about (Romans 12:3) nor hidden under a bushel (Mark 4:21); (5) as "members one of another" (Romans 12:5), we are to use our gifts "to equip the saints for the work of ministry, for building up the body of Christ" (Ephesians 4:12).

Now turn to a consideration of Romans 12:9-12. Describe the situation of division and distrust in the Roman house churches that called for Paul's emphasis on an ethic of love and reconciliation. (Note: You may wish to look back at earlier lessons.) Distribute paper and pencils to the group members. As you read aloud these verses in several versions, ask the group to record the qualities of loving relationships that Paul mentions. List these qualities on a chalkboard or on a large sheet of paper as the group members report what they have written. Ask: *Which of these virtues are present in our list of gifts found in this group? Which are hardest to practice and why?*

What situations are we now facing in our lives, in our church, and in our community in which these attributes are needed? (Situations of marital or family discord, labor-management disputes, congregational disagreement, division between old and new members, disappointment over decline in membership, or disillusionment with unethical behavior could be mentioned.)

Draw on the explanation in "Hearing the Word" above for scriptural grounding for the qualities needed in dealing with these situations.

In the student book section entitled "Why Give People Gifts?" [pages 61–62], we read that we Protestants sometimes overemphasize justification by faith alone to the neglect of the importance of righteous living. The balance between faith and works in Romans is made clear in Chapter 12, with its stress on reconciling love and the use of gifts for service in response to God's grace. Ask the question from the student book that closes the section: *"Considering the gifts you have, what kinds of 'work' could you do for Christ?"*

Refer to the lists of gifts and needs on the chalkboard or large sheet of paper; lead the group members in deciding on a project or effort they might make to employ their gifts in meeting a significant need. Set goals, make plans, fix dates, and choose leadership to ensure that the project will actually be carried out.

Close by having the group sing "Canticle of Love" or "Take My Life, and Let It Be." Then use the following litany:

Leader: reads the list of needs on the chalkboard or large piece of paper, one by one.
Group: after each need responds with: "This is our calling, O God."
Leader: reads the list of gifts, one by one.
Group: after each gift, responds with: "We offer this to you, O God."
Leader: names the project the group has agreed to take on.

Group: responds with: "Take my life, and let it be consecrated, Lord, to Thee."

[1] From *The New Testament in Modern English,* revised edition, by J.B. Phillips. © J.B. Phillips 1958, 1960, 1972. Used by permission of Macmillan Publishing Co., Inc.

[2] From *Romans,* by Robert Jewett, Volume 20 in the Cokesbury Basic Bible Commentary (Graded Press, 1988); page 120.

[3] From *Romans,* by Robert Jewett; page 124.

[4] From *The New Testament in Modern English,* revised edition, by J.B. Phillips.

[5] Quoted in *Like Grains of Wheat,* by Margaret Swedish (Religious Task Force on Central America, 1989); page 68.

[6] Quoted in *Like Grains of Wheat,* by Margaret Swedish; page 68.

[7] Quoted in *Like Grains of Wheat,* by Margaret Swedish; page 70.

[8] Quoted in *Like Grains of Wheat,* by Margaret Swedish; page 72.

TRY ANOTHER METHOD

■ Assign the sections of Romans 12—verses 1-2, 3-8, 9-13, 14-18 (or 21)—to small groups; then ask each group to "translate" their verses into words that meet two criteria: (1) faithful to the original intent and (2) meaningful to "our people," however they wish to define this. After-ten-to-twelve minutes, have group members read their "translations" aloud, comparing them with the versions you have brought to the session.

Now send the group members back into their small groups to discuss the following questions: *How can we put this message into practice (a) in our personal lives, (b) in the situation or situations our congregation is currently facing, and (c) in relation to the needs of our community and world?*

What are the obstacles to and supports for this happening?

Have the members first list obstacles and supports in two columns on a piece of paper and then discuss ways of removing the obstructions so the enabling forces can be utilized for expressions of practical grace. This is called "force-field analysis." Have each small group share their findings with the entire group.

For the naming of personal gifts, use an exercise called "strength bombardment." Place the chairs in a circle, with one in the center. Have members take turns sitting in the center while the rest call out all the gifts of the person in the center.

A variation of this is to give each member enough 3 x 5 cards to give one to each other person in the group. Have them write a member's name on each card and then list on that card the gifts of that person. Next, pass all cards to the member whose name appears on them and have each read out the gifts that the other members have named.

Because we in the church tend to be too modest about our gifts, often out of a false sense of humility, this exercise helps us to be honest about the abilities God has given us, helps us claim our gifts, and helps us from henceforth to be more intentional about developing and using them.

Chapter **Eight**

LIVING FOR OTHERS

PURPOSE

To explore guidelines for responsible Christian living within the community of faith

BIBLE PASSAGE

Romans 14:7-19
Background: Romans 14

> ### CORE VERSE
> Let us then pursue what makes for peace and for mutual upbuilding. (Romans 14:19)

GET READY

■ Read Romans 13:1–15:13 to get an overview of the practical issues facing the church in Rome that Paul addresses near the end of his letter. Then focus on the issue in Romans 14:7-19 of eating meat offered to idols by reading one or more commentaries about the passage.

Pray that God will guide you in bringing home the emphasis in this lesson on responsible Christian living and in helping the group members carry it out in their everyday lives.

BIBLE BACKGROUND

■ In Romans 13:1–15:13, Paul deals with some tough issues confronting the Christians in Rome. Romans 13:1-7 addresses proper relations with the Roman authorities, perhaps in light of the recent exile of Jews, including Jewish Christians, under the Emperor Claudius. Verses 8-10 define the balance of love and law in the Christian life, and the rest of Chapter 13 sets out the moral standards for the last days prior to Christ's return. In Romans 15:1-6, Paul describes the qualities of the house churches as Christian communities, stressing tolerance of the strong for the weak and support for the neighbor. In concluding the ethical section in Romans 15:7-13, Paul emphasizes that the gospel is for both Jew and Gentile and prays for God's blessing of joy, peace, and hope on all in the power of the Holy Spirit.

Chapter 14, coming at the heart of this ethical section, offers guidelines for the behavior of both "the weak" (traditionalists, who believe that observance of the Jewish law is essential to salvation) and "the strong" (progressives, who stress freedom in Christ and living by grace through faith). While the focal issue is eating meat offered to idols, the larger principle is mutual tolerance and respect for differences of opinion in matters of faith and morality.

Verses 1-4 of Chapter 14 encourage the Gentile Christians who have remained in Rome to be sensitive to the Jewish Christians who are returning. Each is urged to be tolerant of the other in relation to their dietary scruples and not to judge others, for God will stand by them. In Romans 14:5-6, the example of mutual respect in the observance of varied holy days is cited for a similar acceptance of conflicting eating practices. What is basic is that all be done "in honor of the Lord" (verse 6). The conclusion in Romans 14:20-23 lays down the guiding principles that one ought not "do anything that makes your brother or sister stumble" (verse 21) and that one must "act from faith; for whatever does not proceed from faith is sin" (verse 23).

The following observations may be made about the Scripture printed in this lesson:

Romans 14:7-9. For the Christian, life and death are not private matters. Because we belong to Christ, our living and our dying are his concern as well. Self-centeredness is sin; we live our lives as an open book before God our Maker. Nor can we choose when and how we die; our death is in God's hands and serves God's purpose. "Neither death nor life . . . will be able to separate us from the love of God in Christ Jesus our Lord" (Romans 8:38-39). Jesus Christ's death and resurrection have made him sovereign over all creation, and we are accountable to him for all our actions. Our behavior on ethical issues—from eating meat to judging a brother or sister—must be seen and decided from this eternal vantage point.

Verses 10-12. The final verdict on everyone is rendered by God, not by human beings. We have no business condemning our brothers and sisters. They and we are equally answerable to God, the Supreme Judge. Paul's statement here reminds us of the words of Jesus in the Sermon on the Mount: "Do not judge, so that you may not be judged. . . . Why do you see the speck in your neighbor's eye, but do not notice the log in your own eye?" (Matthew 7:1-3). The Bible is very clear that only God is entitled to sit in the judgment seat and that being judgmental of others can bring a greater judgment upon us.

In verse 11, Paul quotes the declaration in Isaiah 45:23 that all creation owes homage to God as the basis for his assertion in verse 12 that all will one day face a hearing before the Almighty. While human judgment is limited, faulty, and biased, that of God is universal, strict but fair, and final.

Verse 13. Paul includes weak and strong and himself ("Let *us*") in this appeal to replace criticism with concern in the church. Just because we may be strong in the faith is no excuse for knowingly or unknowingly tripping up a weaker companion. Blithely eating meat offered to idols (contemporary parallels might include smoking or drinking alcohol) with no thought for its effect on the self-esteem, well-being, or faith of another is irresponsible.

Verse 14. Paul clearly counts himself among "the strong" who are convinced that because the pagan idols represent no reality beyond the stuff they are made of, meat offered to them has not been contaminated and thus can be eaten with a clear conscience. "To the pure all things are pure," as he puts it in Titus 1:15. However, this statement does not affirm the old adage that "nothing is good or ill, but thinking makes it so." The focus is rather on taboos that keep people in bondage to fear and custom.

In reproving the Pharisees for "rejecting the commandment of God in order to keep your tradition," Jesus remarks, "There is nothing outside a person that by going in can defile, but the things that come out are what defile" (Mark 7:9, 15). But those who believe that certain things or acts are bad in themselves can be upset by those who, claiming to be saved by Christ, continue to partake of them.

Verse 15. So out of regard for all "for whom Christ died," Paul urges that we abstain from the questionable behavior. We must not let our example cause harm to a single precious soul. We must not weaken the conscience of another. Paul is basing this ethical advice on his theological argument in the earlier chapters. God's grace in Christ has made us free of bondage to the law. In response to this gift, our lives are to be grounded in love. Our freedom in Christ is complete but must not violate the principle of love. So, in gratitude for God's love, we will refrain from behavior that might offend the conscience or threaten the salvation of anyone for whom Christ died.

Verse 16. J.B. Phillips translates this as "you mustn't let something that is all right for you look like an evil practice to somebody else."[1] By insisting on our right to do as we please because Christ has made us free, we could let ourselves in for some damaging criticism. So out of concern for our own reputation as well as concern for the needs of our sisters and brothers, we do well to avoid questionable conduct. But it is not just our personal reputation and our relationships with others that are at stake. The witness of the whole church could be damaged if we participate in something that the church is thought to stand against and if we express our lack of concern for weaker members of the fellowship by doing so.

Verses 17-18. Verse 17 offers a third reason for circumspect behavior. The reign of God is concerned with much bigger matters than taboos and dietary customs. We should not waste our time quibbling about these things but rather join the Holy Spirit in the work that brings justice, peace, and joy to the world. Like many of us, the Roman Christians had lost sight of the forest for the trees. They and we tend to get bogged down in disputes over who holds the keys to the kitchen cupboards, who chooses the hymns for Sunday worship, or who chooses the color of the church carpet when the Spirit of God is calling us into a mission that will turn the world upside down (Acts 17:6).

When we are committed to serving Christ by helping bring righteousness, peace, and joy into the world, we will meet both divine and human approval. This reminds us of the words God spoke through Amos:

> I hate, I despite your festivals,
>   and I take no delight in your
>   solemn assemblies.
> Even though you offer me your
>   burnt offerings . . .
>   I will not accept them. . . .
> Take away from me the noise of your songs. . . .
> But let justice roll down like waters,
>   and righteousness like an
>   ever-flowing stream.
>
> (Amos 5:21-24)

Service to God and others, not observance of ritual requirements, is the true test of Christian discipleship.

Verse 19. Thus we must focus our attention on the things that bring harmony to and uplift the faith community and those it influences. Paul began this letter with the greeting, "Grace to you and peace from God our Father and the Lord Jesus Christ" (Romans 1:7). And now at the end, he calls the Roman Christians to live with one another in the peace they have received from God. Petty disputes, questionable behavior, and judgmental attitudes undermine peace and deny the gift of grace. In reminding them—and us—of who and whose we are, Paul is calling us to put first things first and to make the well-being of the church and the strengthening of its witness our top priority.

OUR NEED

■ When I met him, Jack was an active Christian and a leading layperson in a small church in the Southeast. But he had not always been such. As a younger man he had had a drinking problem. As an alcoholic he still went to church occasionally—even with a hangover—but could not wait to get home to start drinking again. His wife and others had all urged him to quit, but to no avail. One night he came home, opened a bottle, took a drink, then saw his twelve-year-old daughter eyeing him. She said,

"Daddy, can I talk with you?" Jack said, "Sure"; and they sat down together at the kitchen table. She propped her chin in her hands and said to him, "I know you love us and can do anything you want to. But the one thing you can't do is let the bottle alone. It's gonna kill you." Jack looked at her and said, "I can stop if I want to." She repeated, "No, I don't think you can."

At that point Jack got up, capped his bottle, and put it back in the cabinet (knowing, he admitted to me, he could have it again if he wanted). He then told everyone in the household to leave the bottle there until he asked them to move it. And he never took another drink from that point on.

This is how he described his struggle to me: "I would wake up at night with beads of sweat—the bed would be wet—wanting a drink. That's how bad I was. I ran out and opened that door; but every time I'd look up there to get that bottle, I could see that little girl of mine sitting with her head in her hands saying, 'Daddy, you can't quit.' And I'd go back to bed. It took me a long time to get over it. But I didn't drink anymore. I started going to church regularly and teaching my Sunday school class, doing what the Lord wanted me to. This was fifteen years ago. Now the Lord is using me to talk with others with drinking problems. I know what they're going through; I know what drives them. And I also know what—and Who—can help them get out of it."

Jack's behavior was destroying not only him but also his twelve-year-old daughter. The feelings of guilt and depression did not cause him to change. The advice and encouragement of his wife and friends did not change him. Even the threat of losing his livelihood did not do the trick. But when he saw in the face of his daughter the pain and damage he was causing her, he was moved to trust the power of God's Spirit to help him break out of his slavery to drink.

Jack decided to live, not to himself, but to the Lord (Romans 14:7-8). He acknowledged Christ as Lord (Romans 14:9) and became accountable to God (Romans 14:12). Jack resolved no longer to be a stumbling block to his daughter's faith and well-being (Romans 14:13). He recognized that there were more important things in life than food and drink, and he devoted himself to "righteousness and peace and joy in the Holy Spirit" through resuming his activity in the church (Romans 14:17). He thus regained the respect of himself, God, and those about him (Romans 14:18). Jack was giving himself to "what makes for peace and for mutual upbuilding" (Romans 14:19).

LESSON PLAN

■ Begin by asking the group to thumb back through the previous lessons in this study and to identify the topic, Scripture, and key theme of each. Write these on a chalkboard or on a large piece of paper as a review. Draw on the following summary as needed:

(1) Saved by Faith (Romans 1:1, 3-17): Through faith we participate in God's salvation.

(2) Receiving God's Gift (Romans 4:13-25): In response to God's grace, faith in Christ has priority over obedience to law.

(3) Being Reconciled to God (Romans 5:6-17): We are justified and reconciled in Christ.

(4) Delivered From Sin (Romans 6:3-14, 20-23): God's grace frees us to say no to old ways and yes to new life in Christ.

(5) Sharing Christ's Glory (Romans 8:9-17): As children of God we share in the hope of the Resurrection.

(6) Living in the Spirit (Romans 8:1-11): We must distinguish between living in the flesh and living in the Spirit.

(7) Using Gifts to Serve (Romans 12:1-18): We must appreciate and make use of the diversity of gifts of ministry within the body of Christ.

(8) Living for Others (Romans 14:7-19): We follow guidelines for responsible Christian living within the community of faith.

Then present the context for Romans 14 given in "Hearing the Word" above. State the theme of this lesson as "guidelines for responsible Christian living within the church." Tell the story of Jack above to illustrate the importance of changing our conduct to meet the needs of those weaker in the faith. Then, drawing on the commentary above and the material in the student book [pages 64–72], lead the group in discussion using the questions below.

(1) *What effect do you think differences of opinion among leaders had on the early church?*
How do differences affect the church today?
This question refers to the Council at Jerusalem (Acts 15) in which Paul and Barnabas, Peter and James, and other church leaders debated the issue of what requirements for observance of the law would be placed on Gentile converts. This is the same issue—with reference to eating meat offered to idols and observance of special days—that Paul addresses in Romans 14. Compare this to discussions in church councils today of matters like the practice of abortion,

capital punishment, a merger of congregations, or a pastoral change. Because we have strong feelings on these issues, the debate often waxes hot and heavy.

The effects on the church from these disagreements might include: causing hard feelings, alienation, or a downright split; disruption of harmony, cooperation, and mutual trust; a healthy exchange of views and clarification of the issues; getting the differences out into the open where they can be dealt with and resolved; hurting innocent people who are not directly involved; and strengthening loving relationships because people care enough about one another to be honest and not to let their differences of opinion destroy their unity of spirit.

Have your group think of disagreements that have taken place in family, group, or congregation; then discuss which of the effects mentioned above took place and why.

(2) *"How do you act when others behave in a way you find unacceptable?"* [student book; page 69].

"The strong" in Rome were judging "the weak" for not claiming their freedom in Christ by breaking the dietary laws. "The weak" were accusing "the strong" of immorality in eating meat offered to idols. This was destroying the harmony and peace in the church.

When we face parallel situations, we may: be equally self-righteous and judgmental; shrug our shoulders and say, "It's none of my business—let them do what they please"; complain about people's behavior behind their back; avoid and ostracize them without telling them why; make them feel unwelcome; go along with them with a resigned "If you can't beat them, join them" attitude; discuss the matter and work out a compromise; tell them it is OK as long as they do not do it in our presence; smooth things over and pretend it is not going on; attack them and try to ruin their reputation; or ask them nicely to change their behavior because it is wrong, it hurts others, the Bible condemns it, it damages the church's witness, or it sets a bad example.

Ask members to think of unacceptable behavior they have faced and to share which of the above (or other) approaches they took.

(3) *"What actions would you suggest a Christian ought to overlook?*
"What actions require a Christian to draw the line?" [student book; page 70].
The point behind this question in the student book is that "good personal relations are more conducive to

spiritual growth than moral indignation is." Following Paul, the central guideline for discerning when to accept and when to protest is love. A friend of mine once moved to the city where I was living and for a month went around asking, "Where are people hurting here?" Then he started organizing groups to try to change the conditions that were causing people pain. The love of God prompts us to challenge behavior and systems that hurt people but to tolerate conduct that does not really harm anyone.

Raise the following actions, and ask the group to discuss whether they should be overlooked or confronted on the basis of the principle of love (that is, whether it harms people): smoking, gambling, sex outside marriage between consenting adults, dealing in drugs, not declaring untraceable income to the IRS, working at an armaments plant, paying taxes, running a red light late at night with no one in sight, exceeding the speed limit, attending a Buddhist or Muslim prayer service, taking home a church hymnal, riding a bus or train without paying when no one is present to take one's fare.

(4) *"What, if anything, bothers you about being tolerant with others?*

"When have others been tolerant with you?

"Does mutual acceptance matter to you?" [student book; page 72].

Go through the nine guidelines in the student book section entitled "Some General Principles" [pages 70–72]. Apply them to some of the ethical questions mentioned above to see how they help with these decisions. What bothers us about our indulgence of objectionable behavior may be that we feel guilty about letting people continue to be hurt and not doing anything to stop it. Or it may simply be that our need to control or dominate has been challenged, and we feel the urge to "set things right." If the latter is our motive, we need to remember when others were tolerant of our failings. God's grace is often communicated through a merciful, open person. We can be such a channel of grace through a tolerant attitude.

In closing, have the group sing "Where Charity and Love Prevail." Then pray the prayer printed at the end of the lesson in the student book.

[1] From *The New Testament in Modern English,* revised edition, by J.B. Phillips. © J.B. Phillips 1958, 1960, 1972. Used by permission of Macmillan Publishing Co., Inc.

TRY ANOTHER METHOD

■ Combine the discussion of Questions 2 and 3 by forming small groups of three persons. Have each threesome choose one of the questionable behaviors in Question 3, with one person taking the role of the one engaging in this behavior; the second trying, one after another, several of the approaches listed in Question 2; and the third acting as observer to note the effect the different attitudes have on their relationship. Then have the group members switch roles and choose another behavior until all have tried all three roles. Finally, have the members come back together and report which of the approaches was most effective and most consistent with Paul's principle of love and his concern for how persons might be hurt.

In discussing Question 4, explore other reasons than the two given above why tolerance sometimes is dangerous or at least not helpful. Ignoring reports of domestic abuse, for example, may lead to greater damage. Or not standing up to wrong could weaken our character and self-respect. Ask: *Is it better for the church to welcome everyone without questioning their behavior in the hope that they will be influenced for the good by being included?*

Or should we maintain high standards on moral and social questions, knowing that this will exclude some and keep the membership smaller but purer?